John Shobbrook was born in Brisbane in 1948. He joined the law-enforcement wing of the Department of Customs and Excise in Brisbane in 1969, and in 1972 he was promoted into the Federal Bureau of Narcotics, where he eventually became second-in-command of the Northern Region of the Narcotics Bureau encompassing Queensland and the Northern Territory. His final investigation for the Federal Bureau of Narcotics was 'Operation Jungle', which brought him to the attention of the Australian Royal Commission of Inquiry into Drugs. The evidence that he provided to that commission led to his dismissal from the Australian Federal Police.

In 1994 John moved to Coonabarabran in north-western New South Wales to commence a career in astronomy, which included working for two years as a Planetarium Director in California. He and his wife returned to live in Brisbane in 2013.

OPERATION JUNGLE

JOHN SHOBBROOK

UQP

First published 2021 by University of Queensland Press
PO Box 6042, St Lucia, Queensland 4067 Australia

uqp.com.au
reception@uqp.com.au

Cover design by Christabella Designs
Cover illustrations: Palm trees: good_mood/Shutterstock; Plane: Yaroslav Shkuro/Shutterstock
Author photograph by Doug Shobbrook
Typeset in Bembo Std 12/17pt by Post Pre-press Group, Brisbane
Printed in Australia by McPherson's Printing Group

The University of Queensland Press is supported by the Queensland Government through Arts Queensland.

The University of Queensland Press is assisted by the Australian Government through the Australia Council, its arts funding and advisory body.

A catalogue record for this book is available from the National Library of Australia.

ISBN 978 0 7022 6324 8 (pbk)
ISBN 978 0 7022 6501 3 (epdf)
ISBN 978 0 7022 6502 0 (epub)
ISBN 978 0 7022 6503 7 (kindle)

University of Queensland Press uses papers that are natural, renewable and recyclable products made from wood grown in well-managed forests and other controlled sources. The logging and manufacturing processes conform to the environmental regulations of the country of origin.

MIX
Paper from
responsible sources
FSC
www.fsc.org   FSC® C001695

For Harvey Bates
and the dedicated officers of the Federal Bureau of Narcotics
who suffered at the hands of corrupt absolute power.

Contents

Map of Far North Queensland   ix

Introduction by Matthew Condon   1

Prologue: The Arrest   11

1 A Brilliant Plan   15

2 Jane Table Mountain   27

3 Find the Bloody Heroin   37

4 The Final Search   45

5 Into the Jungle   51

6 No Further Action   59

7 The Investigation   71

8 The Triumvirate   85

9 The Milligan Tapes   95

10 The Record of Interview   105

11 Disbanded   115

12 The Public Hearings   127

13 Just Two Simple Farmers   141

14 The Werin Street Incident   149

15 Sentenced   155

16 The Findings   161

17 The End   171

Afterword by Quentin Dempster   187

Author's Note   207

Acknowledgements   211

Where Are They Now?   215

Further Reading   221

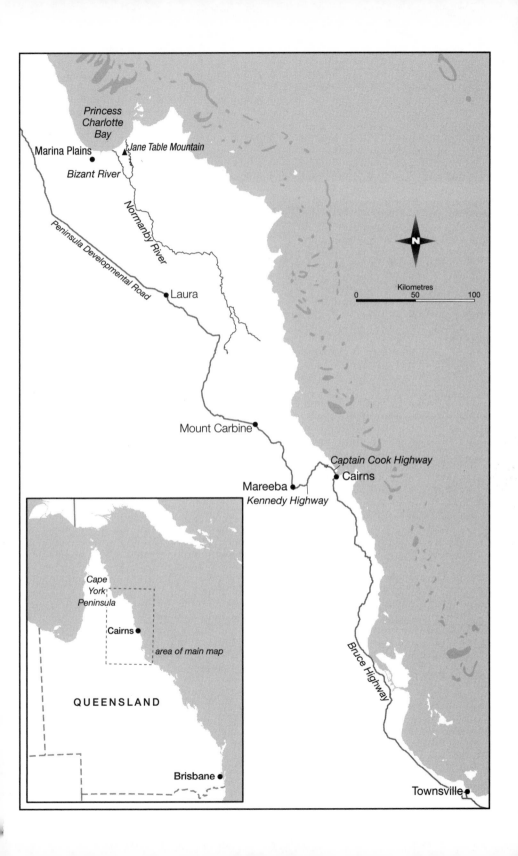

Princess
Charlotte
Bay

Jane Table Mountain

Marina Plains

Bizant River

Normanby River

Peninsula Developmental Road

Laura

Mount Carbine

Captain Cook Highway

Cairns

Mareeba

Kennedy Highway

Bruce Highway

Townsville

Kilometres
0   50   100

Cape
York
Peninsula

Cairns

area of main map

QUEENSLAND

Brisbane

Introduction

by Matthew Condon

JUST MONTHS AFTER DOUGLAS John Shobbrook was born and quickly adopted out into the world in the late autumn of 1948, the pieces of a great and corrupt machine were quietly moving into place.

At the brown-brick police depot on Petrie Terrace, in Brisbane's inner west, a young man named Terence Murray Lewis started his nine-week training course to become a Queensland police officer. Lewis, then twenty, lived at the police barracks for the duration of the course, and bragged to fellow trainees about his hopes of being posted to a country town as soon as possible, where he could cop a sling-back from SP bookmakers.

Down at the Criminal Investigation Branch (CIB), in an old former church building at the corner of Elizabeth and George streets, Sub-Inspector Frank Bischof, known as 'The Big Fella', had established himself as the state's leading detective, with an almost-perfect murder resolution sheet. Bischof had steadily risen through the ranks despite his penchant for shortcuts and fabricating evidence. He was a chronic gambler and excessive drinker, and he had a keen eye for illicit cash.

Bischof had learnt a lot during World War II – about graft, protection kick-backs and how to get away with police corruption – when thousands of American troops were stationed in his city to defend the so-called Brisbane Line and American General Douglas MacArthur had his headquarters in Edward Street. Bischof, however, had become enmeshed in the city's sly grog rackets, illegal gambling dens and lucrative prostitution parlours. He would take those skills, learnt in times of an enforced black market, into the future.

Also at the CIB in the late 1940s was a young detective named Tony Murphy, who was a rapidly ascending star in the force at the time Shobbrook was taken in by his adoptive parents, Alfred and Sarah Shobbrook, and settled in Anglesey Street in Kangaroo Point.

Before Shobbrook turned one, another officer completed his training at the Queensland police barracks: Jack 'The Bagman' Herbert. Herbert would later help mastermind a corrupt system within the police force known as 'The Joke'. Begun as a means of securing ready cash through bribe money, The Joke would creep like a virus through almost every part of Queensland life.

Shortly after Herbert began his calisthenics and legal exams at the Petrie barracks, while young Shobbrook was not yet old enough to attend primary school, the final piece in the puzzle was installed. Glendon Patrick Hallahan, a former cane-cutter and Royal Australian Air Force aircraft apprentice, joined the force. He could have been a son to Bischof; both men were born in Toowoomba, and they shared a taste for fancy clothes and for the retrospective invention of evidence to suit a crime.

The insidious machine, with its cabal of compliant, corrupt officers, was beginning to hum.

Shobbrook was ten years old – a child enjoying the spectacle of the annual Royal Exhibition, or Ekka, with its strawberry-topped ice creams and showbags – when Bischof was elevated to the police commissionership, and his 'boys', as he called them – Lewis, Murphy and Hallahan – became his fully fledged partners in crime. The trio became known as 'the Rat Pack'.

As Shobbrook was being thrilled by the wood-chopping events and Sideshow Alley, Lewis was on duty patrolling the Bowen Hills show site. They may have passed each other in the crowd. At the same time, local prostitute Shirley Brifman was earning a quid off the travelling carneys – show time was always a busy week and a half for the working girls of the city. Brifman would become close to both Murphy and Hallahan, and pay money to them for protection. She would also play an instrumental role as a police informant, keeping Bischof and the Rat Pack in touch with local crime and underworld machinations interstate.

Bischof relished his position of power as commissioner, and over time refined The Joke to perfection. The tank stream beneath his longevity as commissioner was the salacious information he collected on his political masters and others in positions of authority. It served him well.

In the early 1960s, fourteen-year-old Shobbrook left school and took up a number of jobs, including assembling household taps, labouring on a dairy farm, and working as a storeman for a company that sold car cables, as well as another that manufactured office storage furniture. On 29 October 1963, as Shobbrook was cycling to the Brownbuilt factory in Salisbury, about 13 kilometres south of his parents' home, the state member for South Brisbane, Col Bennett, triggered mayhem when he stood up in parliament and issued a damning indictment of the Queensland police.

On that famous day, Bennett said, 'I believe we have a large body of men in the Queensland Police Force in whom we can have only the greatest of pride; but I further believe that those men, in the carrying out of their tasks, are being frustrated, disconcerted and disillusioned, first of all, through the lack of attention by the Government and the Cabinet, and secondly, by the example that is set for them by the top echelon of the Police Force.'

Bennett's aim was to expose Bischof and his Rat Pack. Late in his hour-long speech, he lit the fuse to a powder keg. 'I do not wish to dally too long on this subject,' he said, 'but I should say that the Commissioner and his colleagues who frequent the National Hotel, encouraging and condoning the call-girl service that operates there, would be better occupied in preventing such activities rather than tolerating them.'

The National Hotel was a notorious watering hole at

Petrie Bight, run by the Roberts brothers: Max, Rolly and Jack. The brothers were friends of Bischof and his Rat Packers, and Shirley Brifman and her fellow prostitutes often worked out of the National. Bischof denied this, although it was said that even Brisbane schoolchildren knew that the National was a proxy brothel.

Soon after Bennett's revelations, Premier Frank Nicklin announced a royal commission to investigate police misconduct – the first of its kind held in Queensland – with Justice Harry Gibbs as the royal commissioner. However, the inquiry's terms of reference were so narrow that there was little possibility that Bischof's corruption would be even remotely exposed. Additionally, Bischof sent out his crack team – Murphy and Hallahan – to harass and threaten potential witnesses. Brifman was coached by them prior to her appearance at the royal commission and repeatedly perjured herself.

John Komlosy, who had previously worked as a night porter at the National, had had run-ins with Bischof and threatened to expose the goings-on at the hotel. He would be one of just two witnesses who agreed to expose police boozing and the elaborate call-girl outfit run out of the hotel. In the end, he received a death threat, mailed from a country town in New South Wales: 'If you value your life, say no more. Don't show this to anyone. It will not pay.' Ultimately, Justice Gibbs found not a single instance of misconduct by police. Bischof and his boys celebrated the result with a boozy shindig. At the National Hotel.

This critical moment taught Bischof and the Rat Pack that it was possible to manipulate and defeat a royal commission of inquiry. It emboldened and strengthened The Joke, enabling it to continue untouched for another quarter of a century.

At this time, Shobbrook was trying to navigate his way in the world, to find his passion, and he dipped in and out of a rollercoaster of trades, from a post office telegram boy to a photographer on a passenger liner. Finally, he found his calling. Back home in Brisbane in 1969, he saw an advertisement in *The Courier-Mail* seeking applicants for 'Preventive Officers (Male and Female) within the Department of Customs and Excise'. The advertisement read, 'The work includes searching ships and aircraft, patrolling waterfront areas, and the examination of passengers' baggage.' Shobbrook commenced his training and achieved 100 per cent in his exams.

Just as Shobbrook entered the Customs department, Commissioner Frank Bischof, after years of poor mental health, stepped away from the job. The depth of his malfeasance and depravity would not be exposed for many years, but he had established a deep-rooted and all-powerful system of police corruption, the baton of which would be carried forward by his apprentices: Murphy, Hallahan and Lewis.

Shobbrook shone in Customs, and was sent to several investigators' courses. In October 1971, he transferred to the Brisbane office of the Federal Narcotics Bureau. It was there that he met his future wife and life partner, Jan Hollands.

A few months after John took up his position in the Narcotics Bureau, in May 1971, Edward 'Ned' Williams, the well-known barrister and former World War II Royal Australian Air Force and the Royal Air Force pilot from Yungaburra, in Far North Queensland, had been appointed as a judge of the Supreme Court of Queensland. Always a keen punter – and a future chairman of the Queensland Turf Club – Williams would have known the obsessive gambler Bischof well.

Shobbrook worked at the Narcotics Bureau office in Sydney for a period from early 1972, dealing with drug traffickers and dealers and conducting raids. But he missed Jan, so they married in August 1974 and settled in Sydney. After completing a training course with the Australian Secret Intelligence Service in Melbourne, and armed with covert surveillance techniques, Shobbrook set up a specialist undercover and surveillance group at the Bureau in Sydney.

In December 1977, Shobbrook's adoptive father, Alf, died. His mother, Sadie, moved to Sydney to live with her son and daughter-in-law, but not long afterwards they decided it would be best for them all to return to Brisbane. They were back in Anglesey Street in March 1978.

A lot had happened in Brisbane since Shobbrook had been away. Bischof, retired and slipping slowly into insanity, was picked up for shoplifting in the city, but the case against him was not pursued. In early 1972, Shirley Brifman had died of a 'suspected drug overdose' just weeks before she was due to give evidence against Detective Tony Murphy, after the then police commissioner, Ray Whitrod, had him charged with perjury stemming from the failed National Hotel inquiry. Glen Hallahan, also facing corruption charges, resigned from the force in late 1972 before he could be sacked.

Commissioner Whitrod, who, after a short tenure held by Norm Bauer, had followed Bischof in the role, resigned in protest in late 1976 following the appointment of Rat Packer Terry Lewis as his deputy. Lewis was then elevated to commissioner, and he immediately installed his mate Tony Murphy as head of the CIB.

In late 1977, Justice Ned Williams was appointed to head a royal commission into illegal drug trafficking and importation, and the connection between drugs and organised crime.

Shobbrook would have his own encounter with Detective Murphy not long after he resettled in Brisbane in 1978. Murphy gave him a call, and Shobbrook walked over to police headquarters at North Quay to meet him. There, Murphy proposed that Shobbrook give him several thousand dollars, which he would pass to 'an informant' who, Murphy said, had information about an illegal importation of drugs that was soon to arrive. If Murphy thought Shobbrook had come down in the last shower, he was mistaken. Shobbrook realised that Bischof's boys, despite their advanced age and rank, were still not beyond some opportunistic grifting.

There is an old saying: in time, the man meets the moment. Shobbrook could not have known that as he progressed through his childhood and into the workforce in the 1960s, and as he ultimately secured a respected position in the Federal Bureau of Narcotics, the dark forces of corruption had always been swirling about him. And fate had decreed that Shobbrook would intersect with the crooked system and the men who perpetuated it.

That moment came in 1978, just as he was building a home for himself and his wife. For this man of the utmost honesty and integrity – a conscientious worker, a dedicated husband, and an individual who, by accident or not, had been born with an intractable moral compass – the sky was the limit in his career as an investigator and crime fighter. It was then that John Shobbrook of the Federal Bureau of Narcotics encountered a drug trafficker called John Edward Milligan.

In August 1978, at the Narcotics Bureau office in Eagle Street, Brisbane, Shobbrook found Milligan's name and telephone number on a slip of paper linked to a possible heroin importation in Far North Queensland. Shobbrook, as was his professional instinct, decided to follow it up. That decision would draw him into the unbelievable odyssey that was Operation Jungle.

This is a story probably without precedent in the history of Australian law enforcement. And it all began late in the summer of 1978–79, when John Shobbrook and his fellow investigators headed north to Cairns on Milligan's trail.

That was when Shobbrook entered a very, very dangerous jungle.

Prologue

The Arrest

ON 10 SEPTEMBER 1979, my partner from the Federal Bureau of Narcotics, Noel Caswell, and I landed at Sydney airport and drove to 3 Darling Point Road, Edgecliff. It was nine months after the Operation Jungle investigation had commenced in Brisbane, and a week short of two years since approximately 2 kilograms of heroin had been covertly imported into North Queensland.

When we took the lift to the twenty-second floor, my heart was pounding. People might not think police get nervous, but we're human, and this was the culmination of many months of work. What's more, we did not know what we would encounter when we confronted our suspect as we hadn't had time to conduct surveillance on the premises. The suspect didn't have a reputation for violence, but what if he were being visited by – or roughed up by – one of his accomplices? Or what if one of his hangers-on was armed?

I knocked on the door of unit 22B. It opened, and suddenly I was standing face to face with John Edward Milligan.

The first thing that was clear was that Milligan wasn't doing it tough. The apartment he was staying in had breathtaking views across Sydney Harbour. You could see the Opera House, the Harbour Bridge and all the way to the Heads.

I produced my identification and introduced myself.

Most people involved in crime show a degree of concern when a member of the Federal Bureau of Narcotics knocks on their door, but Milligan didn't appear nervous at all; it was as though he'd been waiting for us to drop by.

We entered, I told Milligan in general terms why we were there, and we began searching the apartment. Milligan was alone and made no objections. He asked no questions, and didn't want to contact a solicitor. He just stood by, apparently uninterested, as we went about our work.

The search turned up nothing out of the ordinary. There were few personal effects, and we didn't locate a single document. The apartment did not appear to be Milligan's long-term residence. The impression I had was that this was simply a comfortable place where he could lie low for a few days.

As I placed Milligan under arrest, my thoughts turned to his impressions of me. This long-term criminal, a man who had associated with some of Australia's worst, including serial killers, was perhaps expecting to be arrested by somebody who looked tougher and more hard-bitten than me. It must have been a blow to his ego to have some skinny bloke, four years his junior, placing him in handcuffs. Perhaps he realised at that moment that this was going to be a little different from the times when he'd been arrested by state police officers.

I told Milligan I was arresting him in relation to the importation of a quantity of heroin into Queensland in September 1977, and that we would be taking him to the Narcotics Bureau offices at Circular Quay. I gave him a formal caution: 'You are not obliged to say anything unless you wish to do so, as anything that you do say will be taken down and may be used in evidence.'

He remained silent.

We took the elevator down to the ground floor, walked outside to our waiting car and drove the short distance into the CBD. As we made our way through the traffic, I started to worry. Milligan was too calm. What did he know that I didn't?

At Customs House, we crossed the fylfot-embossed tiled floor, took the lift up to the second floor and arrived at an interview room furnished with a table and two wooden chairs. I removed Milligan's handcuffs, then asked another agent to keep an eye on him while I debriefed a couple of the senior Narcotics Bureau staff, who hadn't been expecting us.

When I returned to the interview room, Milligan was seated at the table. I confirmed that he had been arrested due to his involvement in an importation of heroin into North Queensland by light aircraft in September 1977. Milligan denied knowledge of any heroin importation into North Queensland and declined to participate in an interview. I informed him that he would be locked up at the Phillip Street Police Station for the night, and that I would be opposing bail when he appeared in court the next morning.

Now Milligan became agitated and protested his innocence, claiming that if he had been involved in any way, he would have fled.

'I know all about your silly little Operation Jungle,' he said dismissively.

Given that we'd spent nine months making enquiries into the movements of Milligan and his associates, the fact that he knew he was under investigation didn't surprise me. The fact that he knew the name of our operation did. But a greater shock was still to come.

'How do you know about our investigation?' I asked.

Smugly, Milligan replied, 'Max told me.'

1

A Brilliant Plan

IT ALL BEGAN IN January 1977, when John Milligan arranged a meeting at the Chevron Hotel in Macleay Street, Potts Point, in the inner eastern suburbs of Sydney. There, in what Milligan would later describe as 'the upstairs exclusive bar', he met Graham Bridge, Bryan Parker and Ian Barron.

Graham Bridge was just twenty-four. Thin, pasty-faced, balding and with a wispy beard and moustache, he looked anything but healthy. His addiction to heroin had brought him to the meeting, but he and Milligan were partners in more than just the business sense: Bridge adored Milligan and would do anything for him.

Bryan Parker was a year younger than Bridge, but nowhere near as starry-eyed, or as enamoured with Milligan. He was a pragmatist. He was willing to do much for Milligan, but mainly to keep his own supply of heroin trickling in from the bulk quantities that Milligan was importing. Parker was also slim – a side-effect of his heroin use – but was not as frail-looking as Bridge. He was also more tidily groomed, with a full head of wavy, near-shoulder-length dark hair, a moustache and a neatly trimmed beard.

Ian Barron was a reasonably well-off business executive, the Assistant National Service Manager for the Japanese electronics giant Sharp. Aged forty-six, he was tall, of solid build, and had close-cut, thinning black hair and a goatee beard. With his deep voice and pleasant manner, he had an air of authority about him. Barron had no interest in heroin. Alongside his business career, he was an experienced pilot and held a multi-engine aircraft endorsement. He loved flying and adventure, but he also loved the buzz he got when socialising with Milligan and listening to his outlandish stories at the male-only clubs the pair frequented together.

Milligan himself was in his early thirties. As a younger man he had spent three years at The University of Queensland studying law. His first flirtation with crime led to him being dismissed from his position as a judge's associate at the district court; he'd been caught stealing law books from the court and selling them to fellow students. By the mid-1970s he had acquired a reputation among law-enforcement agencies as a drug dealer, although there weren't many arrests or convictions associated with his name. This appeared to be due to Milligan's ability to get almost any charge against him eventually dismissed, including a charge of selling heroin in 1972, and a later charge of armed robbery. The word was that Milligan had 'contacts'. Indeed, he kept a comprehensive card-file system recording the details of every person he had met who might prove 'worthwhile' at some time in the future.

Milligan certainly wasn't a 'rough crim', and he didn't use heroin. He was in it partly for the lifestyle that the ill-gotten money provided, but perhaps more influential was his desire to prove his superior intellect, and the thrill of the high that he received from a successful importation. He was a well-spoken man of average size and weight, slim, and with sandy, thinning hair, and was well educated and almost always neatly dressed. He was flamboyant and hyperactive, and apparently had an IQ approaching genius level. He had bravado and a manipulative personality, and he used his sharp mind to ingratiate himself with major criminals and police officers with dubious reputations. It didn't take long for Milligan to acquire his own band of petty criminals willing to do his bidding.

Each man at the Chevron Hotel meeting had specific skills that he would contribute to the group's overall objective, which was to import a staggering $1.5 million worth of heroin into Australia by light aircraft.*

Milligan was the mastermind of the plan. He'd successfully imported heroin more than once previously, but never by light aircraft, and his previous schemes had never had the potential to grow into ongoing multimillion-dollar importations.

---

* The value of $1.5 million is an estimate of the 'street value' of the drugs in the mid-1970s (the equivalent of approximately $8.5 million in present-day currency). Milligan never revealed how much they had paid for the heroin.

Barron's role was to pilot the light aircraft they would use to import the drugs. Barron had told Milligan that he loved flying and had a craving for adventure, and that if Milligan's plan didn't fulfil both desires, then nothing would. But Barron also supplied the perfect cover story for a flight from North Queensland to Papua New Guinea and back. It was entirely plausible that a senior executive from Sharp Electronics would be looking into the feasibility of establishing a sales office in New Guinea, and the use of a light aircraft to ferry staff back and forth as required.

Bryan Parker had long-established and trusted contacts with heroin suppliers in Bangkok. He had never purchased heroin in such large quantities previously, but his suppliers assured him that they could supply up to 2 kilograms with no problems. Parker would also perform the required 'quality assurance' tests when the drugs were handed over. He would then courier the drugs out of Thailand and into Papua New Guinea.

Graham Bridge had no special role to fulfil on his own, but he would support Parker and – more importantly – Milligan. As Milligan's lover, he would stay close and offer the emotional support that the high-strung Milligan would need.

In broad terms, the agreed plan was that Parker would fly to Bangkok, purchase the heroin, conceal it in a false-bottomed suitcase and fly it to Port Moresby. He would then leave the suitcase in the hotel's luggage storage room and fly back to Australia. Ian Barron would obtain a twin-engine light aircraft in Cairns and (supposedly on behalf of Sharp Electronics) 'test-fly' it to New Guinea. After departing Cairns, Barron would make an unscheduled stop at the isolated Mount Carbine airstrip to pick up Bryan Parker. In New Guinea, Parker would collect the suitcase containing the heroin and return with it to Barron's light aircraft. They would then fly back together to North Queensland, where Parker and the heroin would exit the aircraft during another unscheduled stop at Mount Carbine. Parker would be met by Milligan and Bridge, who would eventually transport the heroin by road to Sydney. Barron would conclude his 'test flight' and return the aircraft to Cairns. The Customs department could search the aircraft but it would be clean.

It seemed a good plan, but Milligan knew planning wouldn't be enough. They resolved to test the plan by conducting a dummy run shortly before the actual heroin importation. Then, if the first importation was successful, more runs with greater quantities of heroin were envisaged – but $1.5 million worth wouldn't be bad to start with.

In legal terms, an offence had been committed before Milligan, Barron, Parker and Bridge left the Chevron Hotel that morning, and well before the light aircraft had lifted from the runway in Cairns. The offence was 'Conspiracy to Import a Prohibited Import'. Once Milligan, Barron, Parker and Bridge had agreed to put their plan into effect, they had broken the law.

But there was a fifth conspirator who didn't attend the Chevron Hotel meeting that morning – the man who would supply the funds to hire the aircraft, pay for the various travel and accommodation expenses, and purchase the heroin. This man would also ensure that neither the police nor the Customs department stumbled upon the plan. Indeed, the reason he couldn't attend the Chevron Hotel meeting was that he was too busy socialising with the commissioner and a superintendent of the Queensland Police Force, friends he'd known since the 1960s.

Following the meeting in January, Barron and Milligan set about obtaining a suitable aircraft for the drug run at minimal cost. Barron searched through copies of the *Aircraft Owners and Pilots Association* magazine for advertisements offering a twin-engine aircraft for sale in North Queensland. He eventually found what he was looking for: an ad placed by Cairns Aerial Services offering a Piper Comanche twin-engine light aircraft.

Barron advised Milligan that he had found a suitable aircraft, and in June 1977 Barron telephoned Charles Du Toit, the owner of Cairns Aerial Services. Barron introduced himself and told Du Toit that Sharp Electronics was planning to open a branch in New Guinea, and that the company was considering purchasing a light aircraft to transport personnel. The two men arranged a date for a meeting in Cairns.

Du Toit was pleased; a big company like Sharp Electronics shouldn't have any problem in financing the purchase of the aircraft. He agreed that Barron could take the plane on a test flight to Port Moresby and back.

In July 1977, Barron took leave from Sharp and flew by commercial aircraft to Cairns, where he booked into the Hides Hotel in Lake Street. He took a taxi to Cairns Aerial

Services, based at the airport, and met Du Toit. After a warm welcome, Du Toit apologised and told Barron that the aircraft he had come to see (registration VH-FAY) was undergoing maintenance and was unavailable for a test flight. He offered Barron another aircraft – an almost identical Piper Twin Comanche with the registration VH-ESL. This aircraft was also for sale, on consignment from its owner, Dr James Peters, a Cairns-based ophthalmic surgeon.

Barron assured Du Toit that the swap was fine: VH-ESL had identical avionics and flight characteristics to VH-FAY, so he had no concerns. The two men confirmed their arrangement: Barron's test flight would be a long trip, so he would pay for his running costs, but there would be no hire charge for using the aircraft. Next, Barron submitted the required paperwork, and VH-ESL was cleared by Customs for a flight from Cairns to Port Moresby and back.

The morning of 14 July 1977 was mild and clear. Barron took off from Cairns, but soon afterwards was back on the ground, landing at a deserted World War II–era airstrip near the small community of Mount Carbine, some 70 kilometres by air to the north-west. With VH-ESL's engines still running, Barron opened the right-hand cockpit door, allowing Bryan Parker to clamber aboard. Leaving a trail of fine dust behind, VH-ESL rose from the Mount Carbine airstrip and disappeared as it climbed towards the northern horizon. Barron and Parker were on their way to Papua New Guinea.

Upon landing in Port Moresby, Barron and Parker went their separate ways. Barron socialised with Lloyd Dippel, the secretary of the Port Moresby Aero Club, and at one point introduced Dippel to a friend who had just flown in on a commercial flight: John Milligan. Milligan, the puppet-master, was booked into the Papua Hotel in Port Moresby. He wasn't going to let Barron and Parker get too far from his reach.

Barron and Parker flew out a day or so later, with Barron dropping Parker off at the deserted Mount Carbine airstrip from where he had been picked up, and where Bridge was waiting. This was a dry run, and so no heroin was to be brought into Australia, but temptation had got the better of Parker, who had purchased a small quantity of heroin in Port Moresby for his own use.

After landing in Cairns and clearing Customs, Barron met Du Toit, who introduced him to Dr Peters, the owner of VH-ESL. Dr Peters was delighted to meet the charming Barron, given he was thinking of purchasing VH-ESL. Barron paid Dr Peters for the operational costs of flying the Piper Comanche to New Guinea – $1,000 cash (which Milligan had given him) – thanked the two men and said he would be in touch. Then he walked across to the domestic terminal of Cairns airport and flew back to Sydney, where he resumed his duties at Sharp the following Monday morning.

Milligan also flew back to Sydney on a commercial flight, confident that the plan was sound and this needn't be a one-off. He wondered how many planes Barron could test-fly before they had to actually start paying for the aircraft they were using to smuggle heroin into Australia. The plan was simple, cost-effective and foolproof – provided they stuck to it.

The day after arriving in Sydney, Milligan flew to Brisbane. While there, on 18 July 1977, he made two telephone calls to the man who was financing the heroin importation. The absent member of the conspiracy hatched at the Chevron Hotel was a notorious former Queensland police detective sergeant named Glendon Patrick Hallahan.

As Milligan later acknowledged, his boss was 'very dangerous'. Indeed, so great was Milligan's fear of Hallahan that he would only refer to him when he was questioned as 'the unnamed man'.

Hallahan had once been famous as Queensland's 'ace detective', but he had left the Queensland Police Force in 1972 as a detective sergeant with a number of serious questions hanging over his head. More than just a 'rogue cop', he was regarded as a vindictive killer who had been suspended from the force after more than a decade of involvement in serious crime. In those days, you had to be pretty bad to be suspended from the Queensland Police Force.

In 2012, journalist Steve Bishop summed up Hallahan's career in his book titled *The Most Dangerous Detective* as a 'story of murders, organised crime, perjury, planted evidence, invented confessions, protection from on high, a major heroin importation, a bank robbery, political corruption, protection rackets and other appalling behaviour'. Bishop believed Hallahan had been directly involved in two murders and the framing of an innocent man who was eventually hanged in an Adelaide jail.

During one of the phone calls on 18 July, Milligan

and Hallahan had arranged to meet at the Travelodge in Kangaroo Point, Brisbane. There, Hallahan gave Milligan more money to provide Barron with additional funds for the aircraft expenses, as well as for his travel to Cairns and back, and his accommodation in Cairns and New Guinea. It was at this meeting that Hallahan told Milligan to go ahead with the heroin importation 'as soon as possible'.

After a couple of days, Milligan and Hallahan met again, this time 'on a lonely road in a car', as Milligan later stated. Hallahan gave Milligan more money – possibly as much as $3,000 – for Parker to arrange an overseas trip.

Milligan and Hallahan communicated again on 26 and 28 July, and again on 12 August, which was the day before the first stage of the plan to import the heroin was put into effect. Milligan was keeping Hallahan informed of his men's travel arrangements to Thailand, and of how they would transport the heroin from Bangkok to Port Moresby. Hallahan, in turn, advised Milligan who to contact if anything went wrong in Bangkok: a Sydney-based man named Robert Harvey (real name Robert Althaus). Hallahan also said that Milligan and his men should never contact him directly from Thailand.

On 12 August, Milligan sent a cheque for $1,000 from his Rural Bank of New South Wales account to Hallahan. He later altered the date on the cheque stub so that it would appear to have been issued on 22 August. This cheque represented the proceeds from a different heroin operation – Milligan and Hallahan's first importation, which had been encouraged by Hallahan's close mate Tony Murphy, a superintendent in the Queensland Police Force.

When interviewed about this other importation, Milligan described how, on 24 July 1977, Murphy had departed Brisbane with detectives Barrie O'Brien and Pat Glancy and flown to Honiara in the Solomon Islands. While officially on the trail of a stolen light aircraft, Murphy had checked out the Solomon Islands as a potential waypoint for importing drugs into Australia. Upon his return, Murphy had told Hallahan that bringing drugs in via the Solomon Islands was a possibility. Hallahan, in turn, had passed this tip on to Milligan, and within a month, in August 1977, Milligan had imported heroin from Noumea, his preferred South Pacific Island.

It may seem odd that Milligan was sending money to Hallahan as part of one scheme while at the same time receiving money from him for another, but the two men were very precise in keeping track of the outgoings and incomings for each importation.

On 13 August 1977, after once again phoning Hallahan, Milligan departed Sydney for Bangkok on an Alitalia flight. Also onboard, but sitting apart from Milligan, was Graham Bridge. On the same day, Bryan Parker departed for Bangkok on a Singapore Airlines flight. It was important that no other members of the syndicate were seen associating with Parker, as he had the perilous role of purchasing the heroin and carrying it into New Guinea.

Once settled in Bangkok, Parker made contact with his supplier and purchased 2 kilograms of heroin. Milligan and Bridge were close by, to 'guard against any rip-offs', though how they would have been able to take on a gang of Bangkok street toughs was unclear. Parker and Bridge then flew from Bangkok to Port Moresby, with the heroin secreted in a red tartan suitcase with a false bottom supplied by Althaus (Hallahan's friend in Sydney).

Parker and Bridge didn't encounter any problems as they passed through Customs in Port Moresby, so they proceeded to store the suitcase with the heroin in the luggage room of the Davara Hotel in Port Moresby, and flew to Sydney on 30 August. On 14 September, Parker left Brisbane on a Qantas flight bound for Port Moresby, where he would prepare for the final leg of the drug run.

In the meantime, Milligan had treated himself to a holiday in Thailand, where he looked up some old friends. He flew back to Brisbane on 15 September and, immediately after landing, telephoned Hallahan and reported the undetected arrival of the heroin at the Davara Hotel. Now would come the riskiest part of the venture: delivery into Australia.

2

Jane Table Mountain

ON THE MORNING OF 17 September 1977, Milligan and Bridge booked a twin room for themselves and a single room for Barron at the Lyons Motel in Cairns, where they met to finalise their plans. Barron, as before, was to play the role of the Sharp Electronics executive wishing to test-fly an aircraft offered for sale – the plane with the registration VH-FAY. This time, when the light plane re-entered Australian airspace, it would be carrying a small fortune in heroin.

Although the dummy run had been successful, Milligan had agreed to a change in the plan following a suggestion by Barron. Rather than touching down in Mount Carbine with Parker and the heroin onboard, Barron suggested it would be safer for him to fly back alone and drop the heroin at a specific remote – yet easily identifiable – location. He said that Mount Carbine had a highway not far from the airstrip, so anyone could take down the registration of an aircraft making a suspicious 'touch and go'. Even though the closest police station to Mount Carbine was a one-officer station at Mount Molloy, 25 kilometres down the highway, Milligan and Barron still deemed this too close for comfort.

During the dummy run, Barron had spotted a secluded location along the flight path inland from Princess Charlotte Bay, where he believed a package dropped from the aircraft could be easily collected by men on the ground. Without checking the idea with Hallahan or Althaus, Milligan agreed that this would be preferable, and the change in plan was put into effect.

Princess Charlotte Bay lies on the eastern side of the Cape York Peninsula. It is a generally inaccessible area, being not well serviced by roads. The spot Barron had pinpointed for the drop-off was Jane Table Mountain, on the south-eastern coast of the bay, a plateau projecting from the plains that was impossible to miss. Better still, on its flat summit was a trigonometrical point or fixed surveying marker, which Barron would use as the precise location for his drop.

But dropping the heroin into tropical undergrowth somewhere within the vast wilderness of the Cape York Peninsula was not the plan that had been agreed to by Hallahan and Althaus. The factors that made Jane Table a good location for a smuggling operation – being isolated and very difficult to access – also made it a dreadful one. The plateau sat in hostile terrain, surrounded by threats ranging from mosquitoes and swamps to spiders, snakes and crocodiles. It should have been evident that this was not an environment in which a couple of adherents to the Kings Cross lifestyle were likely to feel at ease in.

Barron departed Cairns airport in VH-FAY close to midday on 18 September 1977. He was farewelled by Milligan and Bridge, who that morning had visited Budget Rent a Car in Cairns, where Bridge had hired a Toyota LandCruiser. Bridge wrote on the hire form that the vehicle would be used in the Cooktown area.

Parker had departed from Brisbane for Port Moresby on a Qantas flight four days earlier. His role in the altered plan was to collect his tartan suitcase from the Davara Hotel, extract the heroin from the false bottom, and repackage it to withstand the drop from the aircraft. He then needed to be in Daru, the capital of the Western Province of Papua New Guinea, by 18 September so he could rendezvous with Barron.

After VH-FAY disappeared into the northern sky, Milligan and Bridge, having little idea of how long it would take them to drive to Princess Charlotte Bay – a trip of some 450 kilometres – hopped in their LandCruiser and headed north.

For Milligan, this was the final realisation of his master plan, and the chance for an adventure in the outback wilderness of North Queensland. Clean, warm tropical breezes, open roads bisecting amazing landscapes, exotic birds and wildlife, and with Bridge beside him at the wheel – what a contrast to the ceaseless wailing of police and ambulance sirens, the congestion, the grime, and the sleazy back alleys of Kings Cross.

Only 125 kilometres up the highway, and with over 300 kilometres still to go, they passed through sleepy Mount Carbine. With the airstrip close by and nobody around, especially police, perhaps they wondered whether distant Jane Table Mountain was the right choice as a drop-off point.

In reality, finding and collecting two small parcels of heroin in an inaccessible part of Cape York was an absurd plan – and the beginning of their downfall. But to the hyperactive Milligan, this was an exciting adventure. A dream job! However, the reality would not live up to his dream.

In Port Moresby, Parker had recovered his red tartan suitcase from the luggage room at the Davara Hotel, so he locked himself in his room and tore open the suitcase's false bottom. Being careful not to spill any powder on the bed, Parker divided the heroin into two packages and wrapped them tightly with a considerable amount of black tape to ensure they would survive the ground impact.

What Parker failed to notice, as he repackaged the heroin, was that a trace amount of the drug spilled into the torn bottom of the suitcase. But it would not have mattered to Parker anyway; the torn suitcase was destined for a rubbish tip somewhere in Port Moresby. Satisfied with his repackaging efforts, Parker left the damaged suitcase in his room, paid his bill, departed the hotel and, a short time later, took a flight to the small offshore island of Daru, 440 kilometres to the west of Port Moresby and less than 200 kilometres from the tip of Cape York. He checked into the Daru Hotel to await Barron's arrival. The island of

Daru was one of the few in the Torres Strait that did not belong to Australia; it was Papua New Guinea territory, and Milligan, when planning the importation, knew that it was unlikely there would be a significant Customs or police presence.

Barron landed in Daru late in the afternoon on 18 September and, playing his business executive role to the maximum, enjoyed a night at the Daru Hotel, impressing manager Marc Seidler with his talk of Sharp Electronics' supposed plans for the New Guinea market. Sensibly, however, Barron and Parker ignored each other.

The following morning, Barron met Parker at the Daru airport and was discreetly handed the two tightly wrapped parcels of heroin. Later, having watched Barron take off in his sleek white aircraft, Parker caught a commercial flight to Port Moresby, and from there travelled back to Brisbane.

Barron flew south towards the Cape York Peninsula. After crossing the coast, he deviated slightly from his previous dummy run flight path in VH-ESL, and set his first waypoint – not for Mount Carbine, but for Jane Table Mountain. Upon reaching the southern edge of Princess Charlotte Bay, Barron looked for the large Bizant and Normanby rivers, both clearly marked on his chart. Once he was between the mouths of these rivers, he would bank the aircraft to the right and Jane Table would lie straight ahead. He couldn't miss it.

A quick run across the top of Jane Table soon revealed the marker Barron was looking for – the trig point on his aeronautical chart. After one pass over the trig point, he circled back to position VH-FAY to head straight for it.

As the small aircraft flew over the trig point for the second time, two tightly wrapped parcels of heroin spiralled down and disappeared into the tropical undergrowth.

Barron had completed his part of the plan, so he set a general heading to the south-south-east, and, after flying for 325 kilometres after the drop, set down at Cairns airport. He parked VH-FAY outside Cairns Aerial Service's hangar, safe in the knowledge that Customs, if they bothered, could search the aircraft but would find it clean.

After submitting his Customs paperwork, Barron had a brief chat with Charles Du Toit about the pros and cons of VH-FAY and VH-ESL. He paid for VH-FAY's operational costs and, with a promise to be back in touch – a promise he never intended to keep – walked to the domestic terminal and departed for Sydney by commercial aircraft.

From Barron's perspective, the revised plan was running like clockwork.

Things weren't going so well for John Milligan and Graham Bridge. By nightfall on 18 September, having endured a day of travelling on a dusty, spine-rattling corrugated-dirt road, they had reached the small Cape York community of Laura. They were well over halfway to their destination, but they didn't know how best to proceed from there – their maps had little information about this remote part of North Queensland. Exhausted, they had no choice but to seek accommodation at the only building with lights on – the Quinkan Hotel, run by John Morris.

Visitors didn't often drop by Laura, especially at night. The small community of little more than ninety people, most of whom were Indigenous, had just two commercial buildings – a corrugated-iron shed that served as a general store and the corrugated-iron and fibro pub. At 10.00 pm the pub closed, the generator was turned off, and there was no more electricity until 7.00 am the next day, when sausages and grilled tomatoes on toast would be cooked for breakfast by a man with hands that looked like they had just removed the gearbox from a truck – and possibly had.

The two Johns – Milligan and Morris – couldn't have been more different. Milligan was tall, fair, thin and trying to be cheerful, while Morris was short, tanned, rotund and grumpy. Milligan was neatly dressed, while Morris's shirt buttons hadn't visited their buttonholes for years. The shirt itself hadn't seen a washing machine for months. Milligan wore slacks and leather shoes; Morris wore baggy World War II–era army shorts and went barefoot. Milligan loved to talk, while it was hard to get a word out of Morris.

Milligan and Bridge booked a rudimentary room that contained a chair, a double bed with a wire base, a mattress that a jail would refuse to issue, and a single light bulb hanging from the ceiling. There was a window with dusty glass louvres, several of which were broken, and no flyscreen. The curtains appeared to double as hand towels.

Following breakfast the next morning, Milligan made a reverse-charges phone call to his unit in New Farm, but whoever was minding his place didn't answer.

Meanwhile, Bridge asked Morris about the rivers that flowed into Princess Charlotte Bay. Morris was suspicious of these two blokes, and instead of answering Bridge's question, he asked why he wanted to know. Bridge said he and his companion were heading there to do a spot of fishing.

'What, without a boat?' Morris scoffed. 'You won't get to Princess Charlotte Bay without a boat, mate!'

Morris had noted that this odd couple didn't have a boat attached to their Toyota, and they weren't carrying any fishing gear, so he figured they must have taken a wrong turn somewhere.

Milligan and Bridge decided to undertake their own investigation of the area. They left Laura and, generally heading east, ended up at the Lakefield cattle station, where they asked the manager, Ron Teece, how they could get to the Marina Plains station, which fronted onto Princess Charlotte Bay.

Teece was tall, slim and with skin like leather. 'If you don't know your way around here, Marina Plains has an airstrip,' he informed them. 'Your best bet is to fly in from Cooktown, or come up by boat. You can't drive from here – you'd have to cross the Normanby, Bizant and North Kennedy rivers. There's a track in off the Peninsula Developmental Road, but it's a long way north of here.'

Not much the wiser as to how to get to Marina Plains in the vehicle they were driving, Milligan and Bridge thanked Teece and left.

The next day, 20 September, Teece followed a series of gates that had been left open and found Bridge and Milligan on his property, attempting to cross the Normanby River in their four-wheel drive. Annoyed at the men ignoring bush protocol by not leaving the gates as they'd found them, Teece told them to get off his property.

Milligan and Bridge's attempt to reach Jane Table Mountain was fast becoming a frustrating failure. Clearly Barron hadn't considered how the men on the ground would get to Jane Table Mountain and retrieve the drop. At last Milligan admitted defeat and, with the prospect of another 200 kilometres of corrugated road ahead of him, he and Bridge returned to Cairns, arriving on 22 September.

Although the trip had been a farce, Milligan had gleaned one piece of valuable information: the best way to get close to their destination was in a boat.

3

Find the Bloody Heroin

IN CAIRNS, MILLIGAN AND Bridge returned their four-wheel drive to Budget and paid the hire charges. They flew back to Brisbane the next day, 23 September 1977, and Milligan telephoned Hallahan as soon as he could. But along with Hallahan, there was another important member of the syndicate he needed to square things with.

In September 1977, Robert Althaus was living in Townsville, and he was having difficulty contacting Milligan, who apparently wasn't answering his phone. When Althaus finally got through, he asked, 'What have you fucking idiots done now?' Althaus was furious that the heroin hadn't been landed at Mount Carbine as originally planned. He seemed to be the only person who had concluded that dropping the drugs onto Jane Table Mountain, as opposed to landing them at Mount Carbine, made the whole operation more difficult, more expensive and far more dangerous.

Althaus's fury prompted Milligan and Bridge, along with Parker, to return to tropical North Queensland four days later. They hired a Ford F-100 four-wheel drive from Budget in Cairns, but they soon returned it, having only travelled 40 kilometres. Most likely, Althaus contacted them and told them to get down to Townsville, where they could collect a boat and trailer.

On 28 September 1977, Milligan and a Townsville plumber named John Kirkwood hired a Ford F-100 from Budget Rent a Car in Townsville. They told Robert Cheadle, the Budget supervisor, that they would be using the vehicle for a fishing trip in the Cairns area. The men then drove to the Townsville suburb of Mundingburra, where they borrowed an aluminium dinghy and outboard motor belonging to Kirkwood, who agreed to go with them.

Thanks to Kirkwood's local knowledge, he, Milligan, Bridge, Parker and Althaus made it to the Marina Plains station homestead, on the shores of Princess Charlotte Bay. At Marina Plains they launched the dinghy and motored across Princess Charlotte Bay, then they travelled up the Normanby River to get as close as they could to the base of Jane Table Mountain. When Jane Table was finally in sight, Milligan thought their ordeal was almost over. Unfortunately for him, the worst of the blood, sweat and tears were still to come.

The camp they set up a little distance back from the bank of the Normanby River – for fear of crocodiles – was very basic; they hadn't been able to fit many creature comforts into the small aluminium dinghy that already held five men.

Getting to Jane Table from their campsite was a physical challenge. In the baking tropical sun, while keeping a sharp eye out for crocs, they trekked through 2 kilometres of swampy, mosquito-infested undergrowth, and traversed a 185-metre-wide tidal stream. Once they were covered in mud, sweat and mosquito bites, the men faced a climb to the top of Jane Table: in excess of 200 metres of steep slog. By the time they got to the top, they were buggered.

On the top of the mountain, there were few trees large enough to offer any shade. The relatively exposed top had helped Barron spot the trig point marker, but Jane Table was massive: 825 metres long and 417 metres wide. The fact that Barron had been aiming for the trig point meant they shouldn't need to search the entire 344,000 square metres of the plateau – or so they hoped. They began their search, but soon it became clear that finding two small black packages on the mountain would be no easy task.

Milligan was no lover of the outdoor life. He quickly became tired of sleeping on the ground in a shared tent and using a hole in the ground as a toilet. Meanwhile, the heat and humidity were debilitating, and the mosquitoes – possibly carrying Dengue or Ross River fever – were in plague proportions.

After a couple of fruitless days, Milligan was keen to declare their second attempt to find the heroin a failure. He couldn't wait to get out of the place, especially as Althaus's attitude towards Milligan and his team was hardening by the minute. It was fortunate for Barron, who after all had initiated the Jane Table change in plan, that he wasn't there to face Althaus's wrath.

As the men motored along the Normanby River, abandoning the search and intending to return to Marina Plains, and from there make their way back to 'civilisation', they noticed a ramshackle camp virtually hidden by the side of the river. It was hard enough to spot in daylight, so it wasn't surprising that they hadn't seen it when they had travelled up the river in darkness a few days earlier. Someone camped this close meant they were in danger of there being a witness to the heroin drop.

They approached the camp and were confronted by a fearsome-looking bushman, who asked, 'Where the fuck did you blokes come from?'

This bushman was David Ward, who was an unlicensed fisherman of sorts. He hadn't been at his camp when Milligan and his band had passed in their dinghy on the way to Jane Table Mountain, and he was wary of strangers – understandably so, given that he was illegally netting barramundi from the river. But he soon realised that police or fisheries inspectors would roll up in something a bit more impressive than a battered and crowded 10-foot (3-metre) aluminium dinghy. If they were coppers come to arrest him, they wouldn't be able to fit him in their boat to take him away. Ward decided that the group weren't police or fisheries inspectors, but they also didn't have any fishing gear with them, and there was no chance they could be tourists that far up the Normanby. He was suspicious.

Milligan knew he needed to take this unknown man into his confidence. He told Ward they'd had a couple of parcels of 'jewellery' dropped from a light aircraft, and they were looking for them. Ward said he hadn't seen any parcels – or any light aircraft, for that matter – but if they were prepared to pay him, he would help with their search. Milligan offered Ward $2,500 for each parcel that he found and returned unopened. Milligan knew he needed to incentivise Ward to hand the parcels over and not try to sell them himself.

Ward agreed, although he understood that a quick payout wasn't coming his way – Milligan was not likely to have $5,000 in cash on him. Ward wondered if he could hold their boat and outboard as collateral until they returned with the cash, but he knew from one glance that the dinghy was worth far less than $5,000.

The men spent the night at Ward's camp, and the next morning the search for the missing parcels resumed. But things went no better, and neither parcel was found. By the end of the day, with his hopes of finding the drugs fading, and with Althaus's temper rising, Milligan said to Ward, 'Phone me if you ever find the parcels. Don't forget – $2,500 for each unopened parcel.' He then handed Ward a slip of paper, on which he had written 'John Milligan 358 3892'.

As the group, now facing the reality that they could have lost over a million dollars' worth of heroin, drove south to Townsville, Althaus was close to erupting.

By nightfall, with few accommodation options on offer, they decided to stop overnight in Mareeba. With just under 400 kilometres still to travel, a break at a local hotel was welcomed by all. Althaus and Kirkwood sat themselves at the bar and began downing beers, while Milligan, Bridge and Parker sat at a table with a couple of bottles of white wine.

From the frequent dirty looks that Althaus was shooting in Milligan's direction, it didn't take much for Milligan to guess the topic of Althaus and Kirkwood's conversation.

'Don't look at them,' Milligan quietly cautioned his companions.

Milligan also noted that a couple of times Kirkwood restrained Althaus from getting up from the bar. But eventually Althaus, whom Milligan would later describe as an ex-army commando type, wouldn't be restrained. He pulled away from Kirkwood, walked over to Milligan and said, 'We need to have a talk.' He motioned to the pub's back door and added, 'Outside.'

Althaus led Milligan into the dimly lit car park, then spun around, lurched menacingly towards Milligan and pointed a finger in his face. 'You fucking bastard! You've lost my drugs, you've lost the boss's drugs – you and your little pansy mates have fucked up everything. Why couldn't you stick to the fucking original plan?'

Before Milligan could utter a word in reply, Althaus swung a punch, knocking him to the ground, and then sunk his boot into Milligan's backside. Milligan scrambled in the dirt, attempting to get back to his feet as he pleaded, 'Don't hit me, don't hit me.' But Althaus began looking for a weapon with which to inflict even more damage upon Milligan.

Those few seconds enabled Milligan to get to his feet and run for the Ford F-100. It was unlocked and the keys were on the floor on the driver's side. Milligan quickly locked the door, but Althaus started laying into the bonnet with a lump of wood. 'Get out, ya bastard, get out!' he screamed.

Although his hands were trembling, Milligan got the key into the ignition and started the truck. He didn't know how to drive, but his fear made him try. He ground the gear lever into first, planted his foot on the accelerator and shot forward, knocking Althaus clear of the vehicle. Then Milligan took off down the main street of Mareeba, with no lights on and with the trailer and dinghy in tow.

After about four blocks there were no more street lights, and in the darkness Milligan mounted a gutter and ran into a guide post. The F-100 was damaged but still drivable, but Milligan had stalled the vehicle and couldn't get it started again. He heard someone running after him and shouting. *Oh God*, he thought in a panic, *I'm going to die!* But it was Kirkwood, who was more concerned about his dinghy and trailer than about the four-wheel drive or Milligan.

'Where's Althaus?' pleaded the distraught Milligan.

'He's gone to the bloody cop shop to report you for stealing the four-wheel drive,' Kirkwood snapped. 'We've got to get there quick and defuse this.'

Kirkwood dragged the sobbing and still shaking Milligan into the police station, where the incident was explained away as a misunderstanding. Althaus saw the wisdom in not pressing charges – a group of men looking for heroin didn't exactly want to leave their names, addresses and driver's licence details with the local police. The Mareeba police were happy to avoid the paperwork and see everyone shake hands so that they could lock up the station and go home.

The next morning, Althaus and Kirkwood took off for Townsville in the F-100, which had a bent front mudguard. When they returned the truck, they told Budget that they'd hit a kangaroo. Milligan, Bridge and Parker's punishment was to find their own way back, but they would only need to go as far as Cairns.

From there, Milligan flew back to Brisbane, where he telephoned Hallahan and briefly told him of their lack of success at Jane Table Mountain. He didn't mention the Mareeba incident, but a short time later the two men met on a rural road north of Brisbane, where Milligan gave Hallahan a more detailed account of the North Queensland trip.

'It was Barron's idea to drop the drugs onto the mountain,' Milligan told Hallahan. 'And that has made finding the parcels much more difficult. After all the problems that we've encountered, should we still try and recover them?'

'Well, you have to try, John,' Hallahan replied in a dire tone, 'because if you don't try, one thing's for sure, and that is that you won't find them.'

No further threat was needed, but one came all the same from Robert Althaus, who phoned Milligan from Townsville. 'I haven't forgotten you, you bastard,' he spat, 'and I'm coming to see you soon.'

With Hallahan and Althaus breathing down his neck, Milligan was duly convinced that he had to devise a scheme to recover the heroin.

4

The Final Search

MILLIGAN'S THIRD TRIP TO North Queensland in search of the heroin began on 9 October 1977 when he met with Bridge and Barron, again at the Lyons Motel in Cairns. They realised that they would have to get creative if they were going to locate the heroin.

The three men devised a new plan. Barron would once again obtain a light aircraft and fly over Jane Table Mountain. He would take a couple of dummy packages of the same size and weight as the heroin he had dropped, but this time they'd be wrapped in a highly visible fluorescent colour. Barron would make the same approach and drop the dummy parcels at the trig point, and Milligan and Bridge would be at the marker, so they could watch the packages fall to the ground.

Barron contacted Dr Peters, the owner of VH-ESL, directly, and Peters told him the aircraft was still available.

Having already 'test-flown' the aircraft, on this occasion Barron just wanted to hire it. His story was that he wanted to examine from the air a cattle property he was interested in purchasing: the Marina Plains cattle station, which had a small airstrip not far from Princess Charlotte Bay. Peters agreed, and Barron hired VH-ESL for the flight.

To the relief of everyone, Althaus would not be joining them. The three men flew from Cairns to the Marina Plains airstrip, where they had arranged to meet Dave Ward, who conveyed Milligan and Bridge across Princess Charlotte Bay and up the Normanby River.

Accompanied by Ward, Milligan and Bridge trekked once again to the trig point on Jane Table Mountain. They had come prepared this time: they had water bottles and broad-brimmed hats, and they reeked of insect repellent.

Barron, meanwhile, took off from Marina Plains at the agreed time and flew over Princess Charlotte Bay. Then he turned and headed for Jane Table. He lined VH-ESL up as best he could and, when he was above the trig point, released the two fluorescent parcels. Shading their eyes from the late-morning sun, Milligan, Bridge and Ward watched the parcels disappear into the undergrowth some distance ahead of them. Barron banked the sleek Piper Comanche and, with a touch of flourish, waggled the wings, before disappearing from view as he made for Cairns.

Despite their best laid plans, finding the heroin again proved difficult. Fearing the wrath of Hallahan more than sunstroke, Milligan and Bridge searched for three days under the sweltering October sun. Ward joined them, knowing that he could earn as much money finding the packages as he could from several weeks of barramundi netting. They located the two dummy packages, and then, late on the third day, Milligan found the first black-wrapped parcel of heroin. Then the search continued for the second.

What Milligan didn't know was that he had underestimated Ward's cunning, and overestimated his loyalty to these strangers from the city. Ward reasoned that if he could get $2,500 for handing over the parcel, then its contents must be worth far more than that. When Ward spotted the second parcel, he kicked it a little further under a bush, said nothing and kept on searching – and he took note of its location.

Meanwhile, Milligan ordered a renewed search of the area where he'd found the first parcel, but nothing turned up. They'd now spent three days looking for these parcels, and he knew they couldn't keep searching forever. Milligan called the mission off and prepared to break the bad news to Hallahan.

Ward returned Milligan and Bridge to the Marina Plains station in time for them to board the Cooktown mail plane, and on 13 October they flew back to Brisbane with a parcel of heroin frozen between barramundi fillets in their carry-on baggage.

Between 14 October and 28 November, Milligan sent a sequence of coded telegrams to Ward, enquiring about whether Ward had found the missing parcel of heroin. The replies were consistent: 'No, mate, I haven't caught any of those fish yet.' In fact, after leaving Milligan and Bridge at the Marina Plains station airstrip, Ward had eagerly returned to Jane Table, where he recovered the second parcel, took it to his camp and opened it – only to find not jewellery but a white powder. It didn't take long for his annoyance to morph into satisfaction when he realised that this white powder had to be worth far more than $2,500.

Ward took his parcel to Cairns, and in a seedy waterfront pub found an old mate named Peter Monaghan. Monaghan was a street-smart petty criminal and trawler operator who had reportedly built and then burnt a trawler or two to collect the insurance payouts. Monaghan considered himself a bit of a swashbuckler, and had even featured in a *Courier-Mail* article describing him as such, complete with photograph, but he was no Errol Flynn.

'It's drugs,' Monaghan told Ward with some excitement. He assured his mate that he would find a buyer for the powder, but he needed to take a sample. The size of the sample Ward gave Monaghan showed that neither of them knew much about drug trafficking. Usually no more than a few grains in a sliver of silver paper is needed (around $20 worth), but Ward, oblivious to the value of what he was holding, emptied the matches from a Redheads matchbox and scooped it full of white powder from the parcel. This was a free sample of high-grade heroin worth tens of thousands of dollars.

In Sydney, Milligan was putting the heroin from his recovered parcel on the market. He made five more calls to Hallahan over the next four weeks to discuss the details, and made initial payments of some $3,000 to Hallahan's bank account during the last weeks of 1977 and early 1978. Later, he would pay Hallahan a further $26,000. In modern equivalents, Milligan's total deposits into Hallahan's bank account were in excess of $150,000.

By February 1978, Milligan was back in Sydney and on 8 February he appeared in the Sydney District Court on a charge of 'break, enter and steal'. He was found guilty and sentenced to eighteen months' penal servitude, with a non-parole period of six months. It would be over a year before he surfaced again.

Peter Monaghan was never one to go to too much trouble to earn a quid, and he wasn't planning to approach any potential drug buyers. Once he farewelled Ward, he walked into Customs House in Cairns and handed the matchbox full of heroin to Peter Gerry, the sub-collector of Customs.

Monaghan knew that the Federal Bureau of Narcotics, a section of the Customs department, paid cash rewards for information that led to drug seizures and arrests. He had made a seizure, and after he dobbed Ward in, it wouldn't be too difficult for the Narcotics Bureau to make the arrest. Monaghan was showing the same loyalty to Ward as Ward had shown to Milligan.

Monaghan's 'sample' was sent to the Narcotics Bureau's office in Brisbane, where chemist Bruce Noble confirmed that the white powder was high-quality heroin. This triggered the commencement of a formal investigation, led in the field by Senior Narcotics Agent Greg Rainbow. Overall supervision of the investigation lay with Chief Investigator and Regional Commander Max Rogers.

5

Into the Jungle

WHILE MONAGHAN'S SAMPLE WAS being analysed and the investigation that would eventually lead to Operation Jungle got underway, I was working with the Narcotics Bureau's Sydney office based at Customs House, Circular Quay. I had been there for six years, and was unaware of any of the events of the Brisbane-based investigation.

I joined the law-enforcement arm of the Australian Department of Customs and Excise in Brisbane on 10 November 1969, when I was twenty-one years of age. On 15 March 1968, as the Vietnam War raged, my birthdate had come up in the Seventh National Service Ballot for conscription into the Australian Army. However, a mistake in my medical examination records meant I was not required to enlist, though I was willing to do so. Even so, the conscription call-up forced me to leave my role as a photographer on a globe-circumnavigating Greek liner, which I considered the best job in the world.

It was my desire to work around ships and aircraft that attracted me to the Customs department. I loved the work, especially searching ships and sometimes aircraft for contraband. I was less keen on searching passengers' baggage; in those days, we encountered smuggled cigarettes and watches more than drugs.

On 11 April 1972, I was promoted to the position of Narcotics Agent with the Sydney office of the Federal Bureau of Narcotics, the Customs department's specialist drug law-enforcement unit, which was based at Customs House in Circular Quay in Sydney (the drug capital of Australia). I didn't love the work as much as the Customs department contraband searches, but I found it challenging, intense and exciting.

It was a fascinating time to be involved in drug law enforcement, as during the 1970s Australia was scrutinising the use of illicit drugs in society in an unprecedented way. In July 1977, an anti-drugs campaigner named Donald Mackay had been murdered in Griffith, New South Wales. Mackay's disappearance had generated an avalanche of publicity, which led Prime Minister Malcolm Fraser to express to parliament in October 1977 that a royal commission into drugs was necessary. 'From all accounts,' he stated, 'the drug problem extended right across Australia.'

Later that same month – while Milligan and his partners in crime were searching for the heroin parcels dropped onto Jane Table Mountain – Prime Minister Fraser announced the establishment of the Australian Royal Commission of Inquiry into Drugs. This royal commission was to be headed by Justice Edward Stratten Williams QC of the Queensland Supreme Court.

It was proposed as an Australia-wide inquiry, but New South Wales – arguably the state with the greatest 'drug problem' – chose not to participate, instead setting up its own inquiry, the Woodward royal commission. South Australia also stood aside from the Williams inquiry, and the Letters Patent establishing the royal commission made no mention of the Australian Capital Territory or the Northern Territory.

Williams had qualified as a barrister after an extraordinarily short period of study following his service in the Royal Australian Air Force and the Royal Air Force in England during World War II. He was admitted to the Queensland Bar in 1946, and in 1971 was appointed a judge of the Queensland Supreme Court.

Whether Williams's knowledge of the law was sufficient to allow him to perform the task of royal commissioner – and, more importantly, whether his values and attitudes allowed him to perform this important fact-finding role with integrity and impartiality – are matters of debate. In his memoir, *An Almost Forgotten World*, Queensland Supreme Court Judge James Burrows Thomas QC summarised Williams's temperament in this way: 'I don't think he listened to the evidence or any arguments. It was more important to him to show who was boss.'

With regard to his legal expertise, Thomas stated that 'although he pretended otherwise, [Williams] knew deep down that his grasp of the law was superficial. Even before he took silk, in difficult cases he would manage to persuade his solicitor that a good junior counsel was necessary. After he took silk he cajoled his solicitors to ensure that he always had backup from a talented junior. It wasn't an inferiority complex,' says Thomas, 'but rather a personal and realistic self appraisal that led him to rely on the talents of others.'

As a royal commissioner, Williams relied upon the more formidable talents of his Counsel Assisting, Cedric Hampson QC. Hampson was a Rhodes Scholar and was certainly not lacking in legal scholarship; he was, as lawyer Terry O'Gorman described him in 2014, 'a "bare-knuckle fighter" who dominated the bar for 30 years [and] was fearless before any judge or government'*. A year after his appointment as Counsel Assisting the Williams royal commission, Hampson would be appointed president of the Queensland Bar Association, a post he would hold until 1981, and again from 1995 to 1996.

The task facing Williams and Hampson was wide-ranging and non-specific. The royal commission's objective was to investigate the extent and methods of illegal drug importation and trafficking throughout Australia, and the connections between drugs and other organised crime.

---

* Terry O'Gorman was quoting the former Solicitor-General of Queensland, Walter Sofronoff, who said of Hampson: 'He was the smartest and hardest man at the bar during his time. He was like a bare knuckle fighter.' (Hatzakis, M., 'Tributes flowing for Qld barrister Cedric Hampson', *The World Today* (ABC), 25 August 2014, <www.abc.net.au/worldtoday/content/2014/s4073791.htm>.)

Early in 1978, following the death of my father in Brisbane, I brought my mother to Sydney so that I could be close to and care for her. Even though she was living with my wife and me, she hated living in Sydney, and quickly became very depressed. Jan and I decided that the three of us should move back to Brisbane, and I applied for a compassionate leave transfer to the Brisbane office of the Narcotics Bureau.

In March 1978, just a few months after Milligan and his team had recovered one heroin parcel, and soon after Monaghan's sample had tested positively as high-grade heroin and prompted an investigation, my wife and I sold our home in Sydney and I was transferred to the Bureau's office in Eagle House, at 82 Eagle Street in the Brisbane CBD. I would be the second-in-command of the Brisbane office, with responsibility for federal drug law-enforcement activities for the Narcotics Bureau's Northern Region, comprising Queensland and the Northern Territory. I got to work straightaway, immersing myself in the Bureau's various investigations in the area.

In the months before my arrival back in Queensland, information had been received in the Brisbane Bureau office that referred to drug trafficking in North Queensland and mentioned some of the names that eventually surfaced during Operation Jungle. This included a letter signed 'J. Sullivan' that was sent to the recently appointed federal attorney-general, Senator Peter Durack QC, at Parliament House in Canberra in October 1977. The letter contained information relating to the drug-trafficking activities of John Edward Milligan in North Queensland, along with twenty-five of his associates. But the letter did not contain specific information relating to any actual importation – only generalities.

A copy of the letter was forwarded to the Brisbane office of the Narcotics Bureau, and on 11 November 1977, Regional Commander Max Rogers, a former officer of the Victoria Police, submitted a report to the Bureau's head office in Canberra commenting on the contents of the 'J. Sullivan' letter, but apparently no overt investigations were conducted in relation to the information it contained.

Then, on 4 January 1978, Brisbane-based narcotics agent John Moller, an ex-Customs officer, received information from a Cairns trawler operator whom he'd never heard of, one Peter Monaghan. Monaghan's letter claimed that a fisherman named David Ward was involved in drug trafficking in the Cairns area. Clearly, Monaghan had grown impatient waiting for the sub-collector in Cairns to organise Ward's arrest and pay him the reward he felt he was due, so he was taking action to hurry things along.

In response to the claims in the letter, and especially the identification of Ward, Senior Narcotics Agent Greg Rainbow, an ex–Queensland Police Force officer, together with Moller and a Customs officer named Ian Lloyd, travelled to Cairns to investigate. They gained further information but made no arrests or drug seizures.

A second trip to Cairns followed on 2 February 1978. Rainbow located Ward in Cairns and commenced surveillance of him. Ward led him up and down a few streets, before turning around, walking directly up to Rainbow and saying, 'Are you fucking following me?'

Being sprung in this way is every surveillance officer's worst nightmare. Rainbow produced his identification, told Ward in general terms why he was being followed, and invited the fisherman to join him on a cruise. Rainbow and his team – accompanied by Ward – boarded a Customs launch in Cairns and motored north to Ward's fishing camp on the Normanby River at Princess Charlotte Bay. Eventually, Rainbow and his team returned to Brisbane in possession of 380 grams of high-grade heroin, with a street value in the vicinity of $304,000. This seizure became the subject of a report submitted by Moller on 13 March 1978.

On 24 April, Rainbow submitted a report to Commander Rogers, requesting directions as to what actions Rogers required Rainbow to take following the North Queensland heroin seizure. Apparently, Rogers never replied to Rainbow's request. At this time, I was preparing for and participating in training with the US Drug Enforcement Administration in the United States. It wasn't until 21 August 1978 that I became aware of the Cairns investigation, when Rainbow submitted a report to me recommending that the 380 grams of heroin he had seized from Ward, which was being stored in a drugs safe at the Bureau's Brisbane office, be listed for destruction as the investigation relating to it was leading nowhere.

For Rainbow, that was to be the end of the matter. But for me it was just the beginning.

6

No Further Action

THE REASON GREG RAINBOW approached me about getting rid of the heroin seized from Ward was that, as the Supervising Narcotics Agent at the Brisbane office, one of my responsibilities was to approve the destruction of drug seizures for which no owner could be found or no prosecution launched. In such cases, the file would be marked 'No Further Action'; from there, it was unlikely to see the light of day again.

When I read Rainbow's report, though, I was surprised that, apart from the actual seizure of the drug, there had been little investigation of the matter. But this was the largest seizure of heroin ever made by the Bureau in Queensland! I asked Rainbow why he hadn't pursued the matter more thoroughly, and he told me that every proposal he had put to Commander Rogers had been rejected.

Indeed, Rainbow's report noted the Narcotics Bureau's lack of ability and initiative in following up his investigation – a barely disguised crack at Rogers. I thought that perhaps Rainbow was being a little harsh, as the details of the North Queensland investigation in his own report showed it to have been pretty scant. But he assured me he'd received no encouragement to continue looking into the matter.

In late October 1978, I went to see Rogers and asked him about Rainbow's investigation, and it didn't take long for me to realise that there was a considerable personality clash between the two former police officers.

'I'm not going to tell Rainbow how to do his job,' Rogers said to me. 'If he can't be more specific in his reports, I'm not going to give him the authority to travel all over the countryside.'

Even though Rainbow's investigation had not been thorough, Rogers's lack of enthusiasm for following up with a proper investigation surprised me. He was the chief of the Brisbane office, so the responsibility for a slack investigation would eventually land back on his own desk. I had always regarded Max – whom I had known for several years, as we'd worked together in the Bureau's Sydney office – as a good and straightforward investigator. His apparent indifference to this substantial seizure of heroin seemed completely out of character.

As I looked through the file Rainbow had kept of his enquiries, I came across a small piece of paper that Ward had given him. On it was a seven-digit telephone number and a name: John Milligan.

Milligan was well known to just about every law-enforcement agency, including the Customs department, and the police forces of the eastern states, because of his involvement in drug trafficking, running prostitutes and associating with hardened criminals. Most police officers in the eastern states had likely heard of him.

Clearly Milligan's name was significant, and made further enquiries even more essential. And so, on 31 October, I asked Rainbow to submit a more detailed report to me, describing the operational aspects of his investigations in North Queensland.

Rainbow delivered his new report the very next day, and I immediately understood why he had been hesitant in giving me the full picture. His investigation had been flawed from the start, and he'd been embarrassingly laid-back in his dealings with Ward at his North Queensland camp.

I hadn't expected Rainbow to knock Ward about, but he didn't have to have a beer with him, or accept frozen barramundi fillets to take back home. Rainbow had made hardly any written notes while in North Queensland, and ultimately he'd let Ward walk off into the bush unaccompanied to collect the heroin. Whether Ward had given Rainbow all the heroin in his possession would now never be known, but I had my doubts. The 380 grams Rainbow had brought back to Brisbane – even allowing for the 'sample' that Ward had given Monaghan – was an odd amount. I suspected the original parcel, before it was opened, would more likely have contained a kilogram of heroin.

At Ward's insistence, Rainbow had written an 'indemnity' for Ward on a page in his official page-numbered notebook, which he had then torn out and handed to Ward. The indemnity assured Ward that, in return for them handing over the heroin in their possession, neither he nor his son, Dave Junior, would be prosecuted for their roles in the matter.

Rainbow had no authority to issue indemnities, but the fact that Ward possessed a document, written and signed by a senior narcotics agent, and assuring him that he wouldn't be prosecuted, contaminated any subsequent thoughts we might have had of prosecuting Ward for possessing or attempting to sell the heroin in Cairns. Issuing written indemnities certainly wasn't standard practice within the Federal Bureau of Narcotics.

The more I learnt, the more I started to understand Rogers's reluctance about encouraging Rainbow to investigate the matter further. But Rainbow wasn't the only senior agent in the Brisbane office; Rogers could have put the investigation under the control of a more effective and tenacious investigator.

When discussing the investigation with Rogers, the impression I got was that he was frustrated with the whole matter. It just didn't seem to be something he wanted to discuss in any detail, perhaps because he knew that he should have put a rocket under Rainbow and had failed to do so. By now some ten months had elapsed since the heroin had arrived in the Brisbane office, and the drugs were being listed for destruction. Both Rogers and I knew it should have never got to this stage.

Rogers told me that, because of the apparent international involvement and the need for officers to travel interstate to follow up leads, any continuing investigation should be directed by the Narcotics Bureau's headquarters in Canberra, known as Central Office.

This seemed odd to me. Every Narcotics Bureau investigation had 'international involvement' – we were an arm of the Customs department, after all, and so the only drugs we dealt with were imported ones. (Locally produced drugs, such as cannabis plantations, were the responsibility of state police drug squads.) If, as an investigation proceeded, the need for an officer to travel overseas arose, then Central Office would be consulted, but it was highly unlikely that they would ever refuse a justifiable request. And such matters only arose well into investigations that began when a drug-related breach of the *Customs Act 1901* appeared to have been committed. Commencing or continuing such an investigation didn't require Central Office's approval.

But Rogers did not appear at all interested in discussing the matter, so I didn't press it. All I wanted was for him to approve my taking over a renewed investigation. In the end, he conceded. 'If you want to do something about it,' he said at last, 'then you get in touch with Canberra and sort it out yourself.'

I phoned Canberra and spoke to National Enforcement Chief Inspector David Schramm. I suggested that if I could lead a fuller investigation into the North Queensland heroin seizure, it would be a good opportunity for me to put into practice techniques I had acquired when training with the US Drug Enforcement Administration earlier in the year. I requested that I lead a small, hand-picked team out of a secure office space. I also requested that no other investigations be assigned to my team members until this investigation had run its course.

When I spoke with Schramm, I did not mention Rogers's lukewarm attitude to the investigation or Rainbow's failings. I didn't want to become involved in a departmental hearing in relation to complaints against fellow officers. I simply wanted to have a crack at what by now had become a 'cold case' investigation. The course that I had undertaken with the US Drug Enforcement Administration had given me the motivation, and I hoped the skills, to take on this investigation. Schramm had no hesitation in agreeing with me.

Schramm wrote to Rogers on 20 November 1978, directing that Rainbow's investigation be upgraded and a supervising investigator be tasked with reviewing the Bureau's information on the North Queensland heroin seizure, and recommending further action. This review was to commence without undue delay. As I was the only supervising investigator in the Narcotics Bureau's Brisbane office, on 29 November, Commander Rogers directed me to carry out the review. Schramm had allocated the name 'Operation Jungle' to the investigation and given it the Customs file number 79/16209.

Unfortunately, I wasn't able to commence the Operation Jungle investigation immediately, as in December 1978 I was appointed as acting regional commander while Rogers took leave. During that time I received a phone call from Queensland police Superintendent Tony Murphy, who told me he would like to discuss something with me. It was not every day that the famous – or should that be infamous? – Tony Murphy gave you a call.

Although it is true that Murphy would never be convicted, he was legendary for being on the wrong side of the law. Everyone in law enforcement, crime journalists and most criminals had heard of the Rat Pack – Tony Murphy, Glen Hallahan and Terry Lewis – and Murphy was the leader of the pack.

I was full of anticipation as I walked across the Brisbane CBD from Eagle Street to the Queensland Police Headquarters at North Quay for my meeting with Murphy.

When I was shown into his office, Murphy began by saying, 'We haven't met before, have we?'

'No, sir, we haven't,' I replied.

'Please, take a seat. You're in charge of the Federal Narcos now, are you?'

'Only until Max Rogers returns from leave.'

'Ah, Max, yes – he's a good man.'

'Yes, sir, he is.'

'Now, look, Mr Shobbrook, why I've asked you to come and see me is that I've got this informant, and he has given me some information about a quantity of drugs that are about to arrive in the country.'

I nodded and waited for Murphy to continue.

'And this is clearly a Customs or Narcotics Bureau matter, not something that our Drug Squad would investigate – would you agree?'

'If the drugs are about to come into the country, then yes, for sure,' I replied.

'Now, the informant knows that the Narcs pay for information — that's right, isn't it?'

'We pay rewards for information that leads to drug seizures, arrests and convictions, yes.'

'That's fine,' said Murphy. 'I trust this guy. I think his information would be worth a couple of thousand at least.'

'Well, we'd have to make that assessment based upon the information and results,' I replied cautiously.

'No, this is good information,' Murphy insisted. 'I've spoken to my informant, and I'll vouch for him. If you can come up with an envelope with a couple of thousand in it, I'll pass that on to our informant, and he'll meet you and tell you what you need to know. You don't want to be seen to be ignoring this and letting the drugs get into the country — there isn't a lot of time before they arrive.'

'What type of drugs are we talking about?'

'Look, the informant will give you all the details, but he wants to be paid for his information and the risks that he's taking, and I think that's fair enough.'

I took a moment to consider what Murphy was telling me. 'Can I meet the informant?'

'Sure, but he'll want to see the money first.'

'Thank you for letting me know, Mr Murphy,' I said. 'Let me give it some thought and I'll get back to you.'

When I returned to my office I sat down, typed up the account of my meeting with Superintendent Murphy, then telephoned Canberra. I can't recall who I spoke to, but I do remember starting the conversation with 'You're not going to believe this!'

The situation was absurd. Why had Murphy put this ridiculous proposition to me? I can't imagine he expected me to hand him a brown paper bag with several thousands of dollars in it and then sit back and wait for his 'informant' to call in and see me. Did he simply want to size me up? I had no way of knowing what his motivations were.

What I did know was that after I ignored Murphy's offer the Queensland Police Force didn't make any sudden drug arrest for which they could claim credit due to the Narcotics Bureau's refusal to act on Murphy's supposed informant's intelligence.

By the time Commander Rogers returned and I reverted to my substantive rank, it was early January 1979. A worrying story appeared in the media at the time: the Sydney *Daily Mirror* was reporting a tip it had received that the Williams royal commission had decided to recommend disbanding the Bureau of Narcotics because of severe criticisms of it by senior Commonwealth police officers. According to the *Daily Mirror*, a Commonwealth police officer in Brisbane had, in a secret hearing, told the royal commission that he considered the Bureau inept, and that its officers were not capable of presenting matters in court.

The Commonwealth Police Force – an organisation whose role had been to deploy members to Cyprus as part of the United Nations Peacekeeping Force, to provide physical security at key government locations, and to provide close personal protection to senior politicians and diplomats – saw less 'court time' in a year than the Bureau of Narcotics saw in a week. The 'plastics', as they were referred to, were hardly qualified to comment on the Narcotics Bureau's competence.

The article was not clear about whether the Bureau really was inept, or whether the *Daily Mirror*'s informant was hinting at a Commonwealth Police Force takeover of the Narcotics Bureau. The federal minister responsible for the Bureau, Wal Fife, had in January 1978 informed the Federal Cabinet quite the opposite. 'There is little doubt,' he had said, 'that the Narcotics Bureau has developed into a highly-efficient enforcement agency [...] [T]he bureau has established an outstanding reputation for efficiency, integrity and technique development within overseas and local enforcement agencies, other government departments and the judicial system.'

As I commenced the Operation Jungle investigation, I sensed a degree of hostility from Commander Rogers towards me. He no longer included me in the routine morning briefings, and he seemed to be ignoring my presence in the office. He wouldn't even return my casual greetings.

I had known Max for many years, and considered him not merely a work colleague but a friend. In the past, he and his wife had even asked Jan and me to babysit his daughters at his home. Now something seemed to have triggered a change in his attitude towards me. But I had a huge task in front of me, so I put the issue out of my mind and got on with Operation Jungle.

My team of investigators comprised me at the rank of supervising investigator or inspector, Senior Narcotics Agent Noel Caswell and Narcotics Agent John Moller. Caswell was a former Northern Territory police officer I'd met while attending the ACT Detective Training Course in 1976. He was a fearsome-looking individual, tall and tough, and a tenacious, hardworking investigator. Moller was, like me, a former Customs officer. He was highly intelligent and one of the best analytical investigators I ever encountered. I had specifically requested Caswell and Moller for Operation Jungle as we made a good team. We were three mates who respected each other and knew each other's strengths, and together we formed a highly motivated unit.

As I had requested, we had our own secure and private office space. More importantly, we were not to be called upon to assist with any investigations that might require court commitments and other distractions from Operation Jungle. The three of us got to work, but after only one month of working on the case a bombshell dropped. Close to the end of January 1979, Rogers called the entire staff together in the main office area and announced his resignation.

We were all shocked. There had been no warning, and no office rumours. His decision came out of the blue, and he offered no real explanation for why he was leaving. I was staggered by Rogers's resignation, but I was facing a huge task to get Operation Jungle up and running, so again I put the issue out of my mind and tried to stay focused on my job.

Rogers was replaced temporarily by Ray Cooper, a sound, tenacious officer from the Bureau's Melbourne office. Cooper was to serve in the position until a permanent Regional Commander could be appointed.

On the morning of 26 February 1979, I met with Commander Cooper, who directed me to proceed with the Operation Jungle investigation, assisted by Caswell and Moller. Almost eighteen months had now passed since the apparent importation of the heroin, so we were driven to put a little heat into this cold case. Unfortunately, that little bit of heat grew into a wildfire, which consumed more than we had bargained for.

7

The Investigation

DRUG INVESTIGATIONS ARE NOT like they appear on television or in the movies. There are few car chases, house raids and action-packed arrests. Most days are spent trawling through endless documents for the next clue, and, in the late 1970s, document searches were physical – there were no computers to help speed up the process. Investigators had to remain persistent optimists, living in hope that the next document in the stack of hundreds would repay weeks of drudgery.

The information that Ward had given to Rainbow, though minimal, was the natural starting point for the Operation Jungle investigation. We couldn't go back and interrogate Ward in depth in the hope of getting information out of him about Milligan and whoever he had travelled with. Doing so would risk Ward telling Milligan that the narcs had just visited him and were showing great interest in the parcels that had been dropped onto Jane Table Mountain.

We believed that we knew where Milligan was currently living. We didn't know what he was doing at that point in time – what interested us was what he had done two years previously. We didn't want to see him, follow him or meet him, and we certainly didn't want him to become aware that the Narcotics Bureau had an interest in him or his associates.

At the first meeting of our three-person team, I summarised what we already knew. 'At least two parcels of heroin were dropped from a light aircraft onto Jane Table Mountain sometime around September or October 1977,' I said to Caswell and Moller. 'A group of men turned up to recover the heroin, and they asked a shonky barramundi fisherman named Dave Ward to help with the search. The visitors found one parcel, and Ward, cunning little bugger that he was, found a second but didn't let on. They eventually called the search off and gave Ward a name and a phone number to call, should he ever find the missing parcel. They told him they would pay him $2,500 when he handed over the parcel.

'As you know, the interesting bit is that the name and number handed to Ward was for John Milligan and is connected to a unit located in New Farm. This is the same Milligan who Brian Bennett arrested in 1974 trying to import 30 kilos of hash and buddha sticks hidden in two rolls of carpet through the TAA Bond Store in Brisbane, although those charges never reached court.

'Ward tried to sell his parcel of heroin in Cairns, assisted by another shonky fisherman named Peter Monaghan. But Monaghan, seeking a quick reward for information, dobbed Ward into the sub-collector of Customs in Cairns, and handed over a matchbox full of pretty high quality heroin, which is in our safe here.'

I then concentrated on our main suspect. 'It was only on 1 July 1977, a couple of months before the heroin drop, that Milligan had that telephone number connected to unit 1B at the Glenfalloch Apartments, 172 Oxlade Drive, New Farm, Brisbane.'

Caswell added, 'If he was one of the blokes looking for the heroin in a remote part of North Queensland, then he most likely used a four-wheel drive vehicle to get there. We can assume that he flew from Brisbane to Cairns, hired a four-wheel drive and used that to reach this Jane Table Mountain.'

'Agreed,' I said. 'Let's see if anyone in Cairns around September or October 1977 rented a vehicle, most likely a four-wheel drive, to a John Milligan.'

In 1978, checking rental histories was not an easy task. Someone would have to sit at a desk at the first car rental company in the area and check through hundreds of forms, and, if nothing turned up there, move on to the next company and do the same thing. Budget, Avis, Apex and so on.

We enlisted the aid of a couple of Cairns-based Customs Preventive Officers (POs) – the rank that Moller and I had held before we joined the Narcotics Bureau. We knew these guys and they were keen to help. For them this didn't seem like mind-numbing drudgery. They got a buzz out of helping the 'narcs', and sitting in an air-conditioned office and looking through hire-car receipts sure beat walking up and down a wharf in the hot and humid Cairns sunshine.

We initially searched for bookings by Milligan in Cairns, the closest town with car rental facilities, but found nothing. We had missed Milligan's hiring of a Toyota LandCruiser on 18 September 1977 because it had been hired in the name of Graham Bridge, a name that was initially unknown to us. Then we tried Townsville, where we got the same assistance from two local POs – and bingo! Milligan's name appeared on a Budget Rent a Car receipt for the hire of a four-wheel drive vehicle.

This was a terrific discovery, but it left us puzzled. 'Why did Milligan hire a four-wheel drive in Townsville?' Caswell asked. 'That would add about 800 kilometres to the drive to Jane Table and back.'

'How far had the vehicle travelled during the hire?' I asked the Customs officer on the phone. He checked, and the mileage on the rental receipt was exactly what would have been expected for a return drive from Townsville to the Jane Table area. We were making progress.

Still uncertain as to why they had departed from Townsville, but nevertheless buoyed by the success of our hire-car search, we moved on to accommodation bookings. Since Townsville had given us the hire-car form, Caswell suggested we start there this time. Our two POs were keen to show the lads in Cairns who were the better amateur sleuths, but this time they lost out: no accommodation bookings in the name of Milligan came up.

We turned our attention back to Cairns, and what our northerly POs discovered was even more than we'd hoped for. Not only did they find an accommodation booking for Milligan at the Hides Hotel in Lake Street, Cairns, but they also came up with associated bookings in the names of Graham David Bridge, Bryan William Parker and Ian Robert Barron.

With the booking details uncovered, Caswell, Moller and I endeavoured to match the success of our POs north of the Tropic of Capricorn. The phone number on the slip of paper that Ward had received had already exposed what we believed to be Milligan's address. Moller was first to suggest the next obvious line of enquiry: 'We've gotta get a printout of his incoming and outgoing calls.'

Telecom – as the present-day Telstra was then known – supplied us with reams of perforated-edge paper printouts listing the traffic through Milligan's landline telephone. We got to work, sifting manually through page after page, until one particular call recipient began to predominate. Milligan had made seventeen calls between July and October 1977 to the non-metropolitan number Obi Obi 25. Now we just had to find out who was on the other end of the line.

As it turned out, Obi Obi 25 was listed as belonging to a man whose career had been described as a story of murders, organised crime, perjury, planted evidence, invented confessions, protection from on high, a bank robbery, political corruption, protection rackets and other appalling behaviour. Caswell, Moller and I looked at each other, and, without needing to say anything, collectively realised that the intensity of the investigation had just been notched up a level. Obi Obi 25 belonged to the former

Queensland police detective sergeant and long-time Rat Pack enforcer Glen Hallahan.

Finding Hallahan's name was an especially rich reward as by this time we'd tracked down dozens of false leads, associates of Milligan who had nothing to do with Operation Jungle. We had even prepared a wall chart setting out persons of interest, and it now listed fifty-seven different names. Some, as it turned out, were involved in lesser heroin importations with Milligan, but our focus was on Operation Jungle. We would get to the other importations once the major investigation was wrapped up – or so I thought.

The thing that staggered Caswell, Moller and me was that the names that were turning up in our vehicle and accommodation searches, apart from Barron, all had 'form' (they were on police databases), yet in all of their activities, time and again they had used their own names. This pointed to one of two conclusions: either they were idiots, or they were confident that people at the highest levels of law enforcement would protect them, should some naive copper attempt to arrest them.

With two-thirds of the corrupt Rat Pack running the Queensland Police Force – namely Commissioner Terry Lewis and head of the Criminal Investigation Branch Tony Murphy – and Hallahan running the heroin importation, there was little risk that Milligan and his associates would be bothered by the one 'real' police force in the state: the Queensland Police Force. The remaining law-enforcement agencies – the Customs department, the Commonwealth

Police Force and the Narcotics Bureau, which only had about fourteen staff in Queensland – were looked upon by the state police as amateurs.

Next we looked for airline records of the group's activities. Fortunately, as the Narcotics Bureau was an arm of the Customs department, we had help in our search for any outgoing and incoming customs and immigration cards associated with commercial aircraft flights. We knew that any light aircraft that had flown from an overseas location (such as New Guinea) and then overflown Princess Charlotte Bay would most likely land at Cairns. Customs paperwork would be required for any such landing, and there would likely have been fuel and oil purchases as well.

Moller and I flew to Cairns and made enquiries at the airport. We were initially disappointed: none of the outlets from which light aircraft could be hired had rented any out. As we were about to try elsewhere, Charles Du Toit, the manager of Cairns Aerial Services, mentioned in passing that he didn't hire any aircraft to anyone wanting to make an overseas flight around that time, but that there was a chap who took a couple of aircraft that they were selling for test flights.

Du Toit took us to his office and searched through his folder for 1977. 'Here he is,' he said when he found the right file. 'We didn't charge him to use the aircraft, only for fuel and oil.' The pilot's name was Ian Barron, and the form told us he lived in Sydney. Pencilled at the bottom of the page was 'Sharp Electronics'.

'Both aircraft sold,' Du Toit went on, 'but they still fly out of here if you want to have a look at them.'

We walked out onto the tarmac and Du Toit pointed to a small twin-engine aircraft, white with green and yellow trim, with the registration VH-FAY. 'FAY was ours at Cairns Aerial Services. She's now owned by Outback Air,' he said. 'That chap was supposed to test FAY first, but it was being serviced so he tested another aircraft, an identical one that was owned by a local eye doctor. That was VH-ESL – she's over there.' He pointed to another twin-engine light aircraft, white with red and blue trim.

I took photographs of each. 'What type of aircraft are they?' I asked.

'They're both Piper PA-30 Twin Comanches,' he said. 'Sweet little aircraft – the performance of the twin is a big leap from the Piper singles.'

'Did Barron say why he wanted to buy an aircraft?'

'Yeah, something to do with flying company executives up to New Guinea and back. He actually came back later and hired ESL to have a look at a cattle property that was for sale up at Princess Charlotte Bay. He paid for that flight.'

'I take it these aircraft wouldn't have any trouble getting up to New Guinea and back?' I asked.

'None at all. Moresby is only about 850 kilometres away, and this is a serious machine in every way. Out there on the wingtips are the optional 15-gallon tip tanks, which ups the total fuel capacity to 120 US gallons. That amount burning at 18 gallons per hour equals 6.6 hours, providing a range of 1,100 nautical miles – just over 2,000 kilometres. You wouldn't even have to refuel in Moresby.'

Flying company employees up to New Guinea could be a feasible story for why Barron needed an aircraft, but the head office of Sharp Electronics was in Sydney – it would be easier, and probably cheaper, to use commercial airlines out of and into Sydney.

'You said you were from the Narcotics Bureau,' Du Toit said. 'We've heard about old World War II airstrips being used up here to fly drugs into North Queensland; is that what this guy was doing?'

'I can't say,' I replied. 'But that's what I'm looking into.' With a smile I added, 'Don't worry, we're not going to seize your aircraft.'

Du Toit smiled and said, 'Go right ahead – it's not mine anymore!'

Du Toit's paperwork, along with documents supplied later by Cairns Customs Officer Peter Nash, showed that VH-ESL, with Barron at the controls, departed Cairns on 14 July 1977 for a 'test flight' to New Guinea, returning the following day. On 18 September he 'tested' VH-FAY, again flying to New Guinea and returning the next day. The records stated that he had nobody with him on either flight. Early in October 1977, Barron had hired VH-ESL, allegedly to check out the Marina Plains cattle property.

No Customs paperwork had been required for the latter flight, but Du Toit recalled one additional fact about it. 'On the flight to Princess Charlotte Bay, this Barron guy took a couple of other blokes with him,' he told me. 'And they weren't with him when he returned. Isn't that odd?'

'Very odd,' I replied.

Having completed our enquiries in Cairns, Moller and I borrowed a Land Rover from the Department of Customs and Excise and welcomed to our team Customs Inspector Paul Jewel. Jewel was a good-natured bloke with Army bushcraft skills – not that we imagined we would need to call upon those skills as we travelled north-west towards Princess Charlotte Bay, but at least Jewel knew how best to pack spare fuel and water onto the roof rack of a Land Rover.

After spending a night in an old caravan at the Palmer River Roadhouse, the three of us passed through Laura and continued north, turning off the Peninsula Developmental Road and onto what were little more than bush tracks and washed-out creek crossings as we beat our way towards Marina Plains Station.

At Marina Plains we met Louis Komsic, a legal barramundi fisherman, who confirmed that this was the best place to launch a dinghy for the trip across Princess Charlotte Bay and up the Normanby River towards Jane Table Mountain. Komsic also confirmed that Marina Plains had a dirt airstrip, which we believed was most likely where Barron had dropped Milligan and Bridge during his 'cattle station inspection' flight. Komsic knew Ward but hadn't encountered any of our other persons of interest, nor had he heard any stories about a drug drop onto Jane Table.

We drove back to Laura, where we interviewed John Morris, the manager of the Quinkan Hotel, together with the manager of the Lakefield cattle station, Ron Teece, and several other locals. It was eighteen months after Milligan and Bridge had spent a night at the old pub, but both Morris and Teece assured me that they would recognise the men if they saw either of them again. Back in Brisbane we had mugshots of each man, so we knew we would be making another trip to Laura to show them to Morris and Teece.

While Moller, Jewel and I were beating our way through the bush in Cape York, Caswell, the strong and silent member of our team, was up in Port Moresby. He had travelled there intending to obtain some routine information, but he returned with the motherlode.

Caswell's purpose in flying to Port Moresby was to interview the staff of the Davara Hotel, and to obtain documents relating to Parker's September 1977 stay. However, as he was concluding his interviews, one of the staff casually mentioned that Mr Parker had left a suitcase in his room, and asked if Caswell wanted it. As Caswell later told us, you could have heard a pin drop. Not wanting to risk contaminating the suitcase any further, Caswell asked to be shown where it was. He was taken to the left-luggage room, where, sitting forlornly in the corner, was a red tartan suitcase.

He phoned me from the Davara Hotel. 'Hey, Shobbers, you'll never believe what I've got,' he began.

'VD?' I joked.

'Ha-bloody-ha. I've got Parker's tartan suitcase.'

Now it was my turn to fall silent. After I recovered from Caswell's revelation, I replied, 'I don't believe it – you're joking! Well done, mate, you've shown the rest of us up.'

Caswell wrapped the suitcase as though he was handling an unexploded mine, and carried the fragile package onboard a commercial flight back to Brisbane. Urgent forensic analysis of the suitcase was arranged, and the suitcase discovery became even more incredible.

Not only was a trace of heroin detected in the suitcase – heroin that matched both Monaghan's sample and the 380 grams handed to Rainbow by Ward – but, incredibly, Milligan's fingerprints were found on a discarded travel brochure inside the suitcase. He and Parker no doubt expected that this brochure, along with the suitcase, was decomposing at some Port Moresby rubbish tip, but now we had it back safely in Brisbane.

Having secured documentary records, witness evidence and now traces of the drugs themselves, our case against the Jane Table group seemed watertight.

By mid-1979, the pressure on the Bureau of Narcotics was intensifying. On 31 May, Bureau Director Harvey Bates had handed in his resignation, although he was persuaded to retract it the following week. The *Canberra Times* edition on 5 June 1979 reported that Bates had resigned 'because, according to Mr Fife, he did not believe the Government had all the facts when it decided on an inquiry, and he had objected to the manner in which it had been brought about and the composition of the investigation team'.

The inquiry was into bribery and corruption charges against Rick Spencer, a Narcotics Bureau officer in Sydney. These charges were first made by drug couriers Douglas and Isabel Wilson to the Queensland police, and leaked to the media by Superintendent Tony Murphy on 23 March 1979. The Wilsons were murdered in April 1979.

The leaking of allegations against the Bureau by Queensland police, and a hastily convened inquiry into the Narcotics Bureau – comprising representatives of the Queensland Police Force, together with Commonwealth, New South Wales and Victorian police, who would act as accuser, judge and jury – had understandably distressed Bates greatly, prompting him to offer his resignation.*

In July, Prime Minister Malcolm Fraser wrote to the minister responsible for the Bureau, Wal Fife, and suggested 'that the government should ask [Royal Commissioner Edward] Williams to look closely at the organisation and control of the Narcotics Bureau'.

In August, the Prime Minister went on to write to Williams himself. 'The Government has recently had occasion to consider improvements relating to the Narcotics Bureau,' he stated, 'including the organisation, recruitment, staffing and control of the Bureau, the lines of responsibility to the head and the Minister responsible for the administration of the Bureau, and the Bureau's relationship with other arms of government. It is necessary for the Government to give early consideration to these issues, particularly in relation to forms of control of the Bureau.'

---

* Justice Donald Stewart, who subsequently conducted a royal commission into the drug trafficking and related criminal activities of the Wilsons and Terrance John Clark, commented in his report for the Royal Commission of Inquiry into Drug Trafficking: 'The Commission considers it was most unwise for Superintendent Murphy of the Queensland Police Force to supply the material for Brian Bolton's newspaper article. The Commission believes that this article contained sufficient material to confirm to a suspicious and vengeful Clark that the Wilsons had definitely informed on him.' Rick Spencer was eventually charged in 1987 with withholding information from an inquest into the death of an informant, but the charges were stayed because a judge ruled the ten-year delay since the alleged offence could not be justified.

Importantly, the Prime Minister did not express concerns about the integrity of the Bureau as a whole, or about the competence or honesty of its staff. But his directive put the Bureau's investigative activities in Royal Commissioner Williams's sights – and he would not hesitate to examine them with hostile intent.

8

The Triumvirate

By September 1979, having spent nine months investigating the Jane Table Mountain heroin importation, Caswell and I believed we had sufficient evidence to arrest Milligan and then Hallahan. (Moller was unfortunately no longer a member of the Operation Jungle team, having suffered severe injuries in a motorcycle accident that July.) We also had enough evidence to arrest Milligan for the lesser, more recent importations, but Jane Table was the most substantial, and therefore of greatest interest to us.

The only barrier to arresting Milligan was that we didn't know where he was. He'd been released from Long Bay Gaol and was no longer residing at his flat in New Farm. The only lead we had, based on general information from colleagues in the New South Wales Police Force, was that he was now living somewhere in Sydney.

We had not sought Milligan out directly during the investigation, and for good reason. Early in 1979, I arrested one of Milligan's drug couriers, Richard Mallouhi, who was involved in another heroin importation. Though that matter was not directly related to Operation Jungle, Mallouhi provided us with an item of intelligence relating to Milligan that would greatly assist our ongoing investigations: Milligan apparently had a false passport in the name of Markensteijn. Milligan no doubt believed he'd got away with the Jane Table importation; if he knew we were on his trail, he might abscond overseas using the Markensteijn passport before we could arrest him. Even putting the name Markensteijn on a Customs or Immigration 'watch list' was a gamble. With Milligan's contacts in police and other government areas, that name being flagged could alert him to our interest. We knew about the Markensteijn passport, but he could have others. We had kept our Operation Jungle investigations as low-key as possible to avoid alerting him.

Now that we were ready to act, I passed the word around among some trusted colleagues in the New South Wales Police Force that we were looking for Milligan. Not long afterwards, on 10 September 1979, the phone in my Brisbane office rang. It was a detective from the New South Wales Police Drug Squad. 'John, I've got Milligan's address for you,' he said. 'He's living in a high-rise on Darling Point Road in Edgecliff.'

I copied down the address, booked a flight to Sydney that afternoon for Caswell and me, and telephoned the Sydney office of the Narcotics Bureau to arrange for someone to meet us when we landed. Caswell and I had been conducting surveillance in Brisbane that morning, so I was dressed in scruffy jeans and a dirty shirt. Caswell was similarly unkempt, but we had no time to go home for a shower and fresh clothes.

We gathered up our files and firearms and rushed to Brisbane's Eagle Farm Airport. As was the practice in those days, once we boarded the aircraft, we introduced ourselves to the captain through the open cockpit door and handed him our firearms. At that time, Narcotics officers carried the Smith & Wesson Model 36, known as the 'Chief's Special'. We used to joke that you would do more damage by throwing the thing at the villain; I hoped we wouldn't need to test out the theory.

After our unexpectedly calm and easy arrest of Milligan at 3 Darling Point Road, Edgecliff, Caswell and I took him to Customs House in Circular Quay and began to interview him. It was at this point that I asked him how he knew about Operation Jungle, and he stunned me by replying with, 'Max told me.' The Max he was referring to was Max Rogers, the former Chief Investigator and Regional Commander of the Brisbane office of the Federal Bureau of Narcotics.

I knew that Milligan delighted in one-upmanship, and that he liked to brag about his contacts and influence, but even so, Milligan mentioning Max Rogers made my stomach churn. Could it be true? Was it possible that Max had betrayed us, and perhaps even that he'd tried to scuttle the investigation? I tried my best to stay calm as I considered the implications of what Milligan had told me; I had to appear unfazed and professional.

If Max Rogers had been passing Milligan information, then his access to information would have dried up in late January 1979, when Rogers had resigned. I prayed that there wasn't someone else in the Bureau's office who was leaking information.

If Milligan was telling me the truth, then it was likely he was playing both sides of the fence, acting as a prize informer for Rogers in order to eliminate his competitors while covertly extracting snippets of information from Rogers. After all, Milligan was credited with an IQ at near-genius level. Perhaps Rogers had realised this too late, and instead of arresting Milligan had decided to walk away from the Narcotics Bureau.

Whatever the situation with Rogers, Milligan was refusing to answer any questions about the Jane Table importation, so my priority was to put him before the court and have him taken into custody. I told him that he would have to surrender his passport, to which he replied that he'd spilt ink on it and thrown it away.

We took the lift downstairs, exited Customs House and, with my hand firmly gripping Milligan's belt at the small of his back, we crossed Circular Quay and walked towards the Phillip Street Police Station. Milligan would spend the night there ahead of his appearance at the Special Federal Court the following morning.

I didn't really need to hold on to Milligan too tightly – with the fearsome Caswell beside us, I doubt Milligan would have tried to make a break for it. And, as

I later learnt, Milligan was confident that he would be freed very soon, and that he wouldn't be facing any charges, as had been the outcome of several of his previous arrests.

Having deposited Milligan at Phillip Street, Caswell and I drove across the Harbour Bridge to Neutral Bay, where Milligan's sister, Meralyn, lived. Arriving at her home close to midnight, and looking somewhat dishevelled, I was surprised that she opened the door. I showed her my identification and introduced myself. I informed Meralyn and her husband of her brother's arrest and spoke to her about Milligan obtaining bail. I advised her that one of the bail conditions would be that her brother surrender his passport.

'Do you want to take it now?' she asked. She fetched the passport and handed it over; Milligan's claimed ink stains appeared to have magically vanished.

The next morning, at the Special Federal Court, still wearing yesterday's clothes and unshaven, and having only had a couple of hours' sleep. I sat beside Milligan, who was, as always, dapperly dressed.

At one point in the proceedings, the magistrate instructed, 'Will the prisoner stand.'

Milligan did not move, and the police officer assisting the magistrate walked over to me, gave me a shove and said, 'Get up!'

Feeling somewhat aggrieved, I pointed to Milligan. 'He's the prisoner,' I complained. 'I'm the arresting officer!'

Milligan was charged with conspiracy to import a quantity of heroin into Australia. This charge did not relate to the Operation Jungle importation, but to Milligan's more recent attempted importation from Noumea. We were yet to properly interview Milligan about the Operation Jungle matter, and our immediate concern was whether he would be granted bail.

When the question arose, Milligan told the magistrate the same story he'd told me: that he had damaged his passport and thrown it away. I got to my feet, held up Milligan's passport and informed the magistrate that this was not true, and that Milligan's sister had handed his passport to me the previous night.

Milligan looked at me with contempt as he was remanded in custody. By catching out his lie to the magistrate, I had guaranteed that he would be refused bail.

Milligan didn't care that the court had his passport, of course, because he still had his other passport: the one in the name of Markensteijn. We didn't know where this false passport was, but there was no mileage to be gained in letting Milligan know that I knew it was out there somewhere.

Caswell and I had successfully arrested one of the masterminds of the heroin importation operation. The other members of the conspiracy – Ian Barron, Graham Bridge, John Kirkwood, Robert Althaus and Glen Hallahan – were all still at large, so we had a lot of work ahead of us. Caswell and I were keen to lodge Milligan in Long Bay Gaol and get back to Brisbane to press on with the investigation. In particular, we wanted to turn our attention to Hallahan.

~

As I was about to leave the court, Milligan grasped my arm and asked, 'Can I talk to you?'

I was exhausted and in no mood to play his games. No doubt he wanted to dob someone else in, to lessen his own culpability. All I wanted was to catch the earliest flight back to Brisbane. 'You had every opportunity last night,' I said, pulling my arm away. 'I'll see you in two weeks at your next court appearance.'

'You're just a boy,' he replied. 'You don't know how big this is. Can I talk to you?'

I heard a hint of desperation in his voice. Milligan was scared, I realised.

I asked the police officers who were about to transport him to Long Bay if I could have a private moment with Milligan in an interview room. Milligan's solicitor and the escorting police officers agreed. Once we were inside the room, Milligan confirmed what I already believed, but I had never expected to hear it from him. And certainly not as soon as this.

Milligan wasn't the mastermind behind the importation, he told me. People of much greater power than him were involved.

'Which importation are we talking about?' I asked.

'The North Queensland importation,' he replied.

'Like who?' I asked.

'I call them the Triumvirate,' he said.

Now he had my attention.

'I report to Glen Hallahan,' the nervous Milligan explained, his cockiness vanished. 'He reports to Tony Murphy, and then to Terry Lewis. I need to talk to you,' he insisted. 'I need your help. If I go to Long Bay Gaol, I'll be killed. There are people in there who will fear that I'll talk. Tell Harvey Bates that I'll cooperate, but I can't go to Long Bay.'

I knew Milligan was prone to big-noting himself and telling grandiose stories, so I needed some confirmation that he was being truthful before I told my boss he should leap into action because of something Milligan had told me.

'Where is the Markensteijn passport?' I demanded.

Milligan replied without a moment's hesitation. 'It's in a room in Paddington that I rent. That's where I keep all of my documents. I'll tell you where it is, but if you go there, you won't charge me with anything else, will you?'

'John, if there's a body under the bed, I might find that hard to ignore, but I'm concerned about the North Queensland heroin importation at the moment. How do we find the room?'

'I'll write down directions,' he said.

I gave him my official notebook, into which he wrote: 'Graham (David), please just hand to this gentleman the key which you have to Paddo. Stay cool & come & see. John.'

Milligan said a key could be found on a ledge near the door to the room, but he also told me how to locate Graham Bridge if the hidden key wasn't there. To give up the passport and Bridge's whereabouts convinced me that Milligan was putting a hell of a lot of trust in me.

With Caswell and Supervising Narcotics Agent Phil Lawrence, I drove to 223 Sutherland Street, Paddington.

The front door was open, and the building appeared to consist of individually rented rooms. The key to Milligan's room was located on the ledge, just as he had described. Inside was an investigator's Aladdin's cave.

We quickly found the Markensteijn passport, as well as several more passport applications in different names, to each of which was affixed a photograph of Milligan. We found Milligan's diaries, as well as bank deposit and transfer slips for payments to the account of Glen Hallahan. The diaries contained references to Tony Murphy and Terry Lewis, and to Bridge, Parker and Barron. Lawrence and I packed the documentation into a suitcase and took it back to Customs House.

As we worked through this material, we learnt that there was yet another address in Paddington that Milligan was using: unit 6 of 19 Cooper Street, Paddington. This apartment was rented in the name of Julal Raad, a young courier whom I had arrested two months previously. A check of the records of the telephone connected to this unit revealed a number of calls to Hallahan's number in Obi Obi.

I telephoned Canberra and spoke to Narcotics Bureau Assistant Director Brian Bates, the brother of Director Harvey Bates. I told Brian Bates that, in view of Milligan confirming much of what we already knew, his giving up the Markensteijn passport and leading us to the Sutherland Street, Paddington room, I believed he was being truthful, that he was indeed in fear of his life, and that he was prepared to talk to us. Arrangements were immediately made for him to be segregated from all other prisoners at Long Bay

Gaol until we could organise alternative confinement for him at a separate location.

It is interesting how the course of your life can turn on one apparently minor event. When Milligan was charged at the Special Federal Court in Sydney, I was delighted that the first magistrate he encountered was honest and had not been 'got at' by a friend of Milligan's in high places. Because the magistrate hadn't been pressured to do otherwise, he did not grant Milligan bail.

If Milligan had been granted bail at that time, I am sure I would never have seen him again. With access to a false passport, he would surely have fled to live a colourful life somewhere in South-East Asia, and the officers of the Federal Bureau of Narcotics would have moved on to other investigations. Yet Milligan wasn't granted bail, and because of that, and my ongoing involvement with him, my career started its decline. Success can lead to failure.

I had successfully arrested Milligan. No strings had been pulled for him, and I did my job and got him talking. The problem was that I saw things in black and white – it was me versus Milligan and Hallahan. I failed to consider whose toes I was treading on. I was ignorant of the possibility that the Hallahan/Milligan group might have support not only within the Queensland Police Force, but within the Queensland Government and the Queensland Supreme Court as well.

And there was no chance I would prevail against that coalition of power.

9

The Milligan Tapes

On the morning of 12 September 1979, less than forty hours since I first laid eyes on Milligan 'in the flesh', having obtained an order from the Department of Corrective Services, another officer and I went to Long Bay Gaol to collect Milligan and take him back to Customs House, where my questioning of him would commence.

It was awkward driving through the Sydney morning traffic and making small talk about the weather and other inconsequential matters while we ignored the fact that we were about to discuss what was potentially one of the largest drug-importation schemes in the country. I tried not to say anything that would upset Milligan; I didn't want to reinforce his opinion that I was 'just a boy'. Talking for an hour when the only thing we had in common was an interest in a million dollars' worth of heroin wasn't easy.

We arrived at Customs House, took the lift to the second floor and entered the small, pegboard-lined interview room that Milligan had briefly occupied on the night of his arrest. I placed a portable cassette tape recorder on the table and told Milligan that I would use this to record what he had to tell me.

Chief Inspector David Schramm from the Bureau of Narcotics' headquarters in Canberra had told me to 'give Milligan his head' and 'find out as much as Milligan wanted to talk about'. Letting Milligan speak freely was a good way for us to break the ice. I wouldn't attempt to gain an admission concerning any specific offence; rather, I would encourage him to tell me about whatever he wanted to. I might ask some clarifying questions, but Milligan and I were participating in a reasonably informal conversation – one that was not intended to be submitted as evidence to a court or read by lawyers. Milligan had morphed into his role as an informant, and he was about to provide me with background intelligence, not evidence, on a wide range of criminal activities.

The informal nature of our exchange allowed us to develop a rapport of sorts. I treated him as I would have treated anyone who was assisting me by providing information. I was courteous and listened to him patiently, and I didn't express any distaste or condemnation for Milligan or the events he was telling me about.

From the start, Milligan and I attempted to size each other up. I had no idea what he thought of me, but he wasn't as aloof or cold as he'd been on the night of his arrest. In a small room, talking one-on-one and not in front of an audience, he could open up and be himself. There was no point in me yelling at or threatening him – I spoke quietly to him and he spoke quietly to me. There was no requirement for a 'witness' to sit in on our conversation, as this was not a potentially adversarial 'record of interview' situation. The tapes would serve as the witness to what was said.

I found Milligan to be a highly intelligent, highly sensitive and highly strung individual. I soon realised that harsh words or macho tactics – which I was incapable of anyway – would have caused him to retreat. Rather, he needed to hear me say, 'I understand.' Milligan was a complicated man. He had the makings of a decent person. He wasn't indifferent to other people's feelings and he didn't try to hurt or belittle people. But somewhere in his past his sense of right and wrong had received a severe blow and had never reset. He would have been aghast to think that his heroin trafficking was actually harming anyone – after all, people didn't have to buy heroin from him if they didn't want to. He wasn't greedy for wealth, and, other than Graham Bridge, there appeared to be very few people with whom he felt comfortable.

During the interview, I did tell him that I understood. I understood that he had given loyalty to people who hadn't returned that loyalty – Hallahan, for instance. I told him that Hallahan had treated him as a commodity and not as a person. I also told him that nobody, not even Hallahan, would be able to get me to withdraw any charges. Milligan and I got to know each other over the two days of interviews. We ate sandwiches together. I made him cups of tea, took him to the toilet, and drove him to Long Bay and back. At times our exchanges became quite emotional: he cried and I sympathised. We were communicating.

There was most likely some exaggeration in Milligan's disclosures, but that was in his nature. Even so, he was consistent in what he told me; matters that he mentioned on the first day he could retell in exactly the same detail late the following day. He was unaware that I knew of many of the characters he was naming, and already knew of some of the matters he was telling me about. The facts that I knew confirmed for me that his revelations weren't totally absurd.

It may sound odd, but during the interviews I started to develop some empathy for Milligan. He had his little group of puppets that he played with, but his strings were in turn being pulled by two of the coldest and most callous men in Australia that you would never want to meet. For years he had put his trust and faith in the assurances of Hallahan and the power of Murphy. Now, when he needed them most, they had failed him.

He had expected Hallahan and Murphy to pull strings to ensure that he was granted bail, and then, using the Markensteijn passport, he would disappear. That hadn't happened. The influence that Hallahan and Murphy had in his life had suddenly dissipated, only to be replaced by the influence of a young Federal Narcotics agent. And there was nothing in my background that would encourage a Queensland or New South Wales police officer to convince me to go easy on Milligan.

As our discussions continued, Milligan seemed to relax more in my company. He was certainly a showman; at one point, as something important popped into his mind, he thrust a finger into the air and exclaimed, 'Evidence, evidence!' He began guiding me, telling me where I could find corroborating evidence for offences he told me about.

When Max Rogers had resigned, Milligan told me, the choice of his replacement as the Narcotics Bureau Regional Commander was influenced by Terry Lewis, with the result that a friend of Hallahan's, another former Queensland police officer, got the job. It was true that an ex–Queensland police officer, John Robinson, had won the role, but I'd got to know Robinson reasonably well, and I was deeply sceptical. He didn't appear to have any of the qualities that a friend of Hallahan's or any type of bent copper would be likely to exhibit.

Milligan spoke of corruption within the New South Wales and Queensland police forces, but also within the judiciary and the government. He named officers in the Immigration Department who had assisted him whenever he submitted false passport applications. He told me about fellow criminals; some names I recognised, many I didn't. All in all, the extent of his revelations was staggering. I recall thinking that the Narcotics Bureau should, at the least, form a small task force to go through my tapes in detail and investigate Milligan's allegations. If his claims could be substantiated and hard evidence was forthcoming, prosecutions should surely be launched. To my knowledge, this investigation never happened.

When we reached the subject of the Rat Pack, whom Milligan referred to as 'the Triumvirate', his comments became more general in nature. He told me that the Commissioner of the Queensland Police Force, Terry Lewis, the head of the Criminal Investigation Branch, Tony Murphy, and former detective sergeant Glen Hallahan operated as a three-man team, and together controlled aspects of crime in Queensland. He identified Hallahan as the man who did the dirty work, and Murphy, not Lewis, as the boss.

Some names Milligan was reluctant to disclose on tape – those of Hallahan and Rogers, for example – but the volume and apparent quality of the information he was providing me were considerable. Whenever Milligan reached a point where he did not wish what he was about to say to be recorded, such as revealing the name of a close friend who may have been involved, he would indicate for me to stop the tape recorder. I would do so, Milligan would tell me the name of the person involved or some other item of sensitive material, and then I would restart the tape and he would continue his on-the-record comments. I was comfortable complying with his wishes; doing so meant I could hear the sensitive material, if not record it, and I could keep his revelations flowing.

At the termination of each day's interview, the Milligan Tapes were flown safe-hand to the Narcotics Bureau's Central Office in Canberra, where they were handed to Assistant Director Brian Bates.

I knew that Milligan's allegations were being taken seriously by Central Office when the Bureau's Assistant

Commissioner for the Information and Intelligence Section, Dan Scullion, flew from Canberra to Sydney on 14 September to interview Milligan personally.

Scullion put his own series of questions to Milligan, but they were based on what he had already heard on the tapes that I had recorded. Scullion used the same technique as I did, with a cassette tape recorder on the interview room table, and his recordings took place over three days. What Milligan did not know was that, for the Scullion interviews, the microphone from a large reel-to-reel tape recorder had been secreted behind a pegboard, so that all of Milligan's detailed allegations, including the 'off-the-record' material, could be recorded by Chief Inspector David Schramm.

Over the same three days, I was also involved in conducting formal records of interview with Milligan in relation to other heroin importations he had organised between the Operation Jungle importation in 1977 and his arrest in 1979. On the morning of 14 September 1979, I commenced to interview Milligan in relation to one of these other importations – the one in which Richard Mallouhi had been involved. Although Operation Jungle was our major investigation, these other offences could not be ignored. As my questions became more specific, Milligan requested that the interview be suspended, and at 12.59 pm I agreed.

What was happening, I realised, was that Milligan was concerned that his answers to my questions were tending to indicate that he had perjured himself when he had given evidence to the New South Wales Royal Commission into Drug Trafficking, also known as the Woodward royal commission, which had commenced taking evidence in August 1977. Milligan had told Commissioner Woodward that he had police and political protection in Queensland, which implied that he was being protected by Murphy, who was head of the state's criminal intelligence section from 1976 and superintendent in charge of the state's criminal investigations from 31 October 1977. The Woodward royal commission had been established to investigate drug trafficking in New South Wales, and especially links between the Mafia and New South Wales police, and the disappearance of anti-marijuana campaigner Donald Mackay.

Following the suspension of our formal interview, I returned Milligan to Long Bay and flew back to Brisbane that evening. In the end, the Milligan Tapes had not provided any evidence specifically related to Operation Jungle; they were Milligan's account of his own life in crime. They certainly told of crimes committed by Milligan and others, but without further investigation we lacked the corroborative hard evidence needed to prepare briefs of evidence against any individuals.

Caswell and I were still gathering evidence on Barron and Bridge, however, and preparing Operation Jungle briefs of evidence for each of them. But the formal Record of Interview between Milligan and me – a major item of evidence – was delayed by the turmoil that the Narcotics Bureau was going through.

On 17 September, Director Harvey Bates sent a memorandum to Wal Fife, telling him that the Queensland Police Force and Commonwealth Police Force had 'figured significantly' in 'direct attacks' upon the Bureau.

Bates had wasted no time in reacting to the contents of the Milligan Tapes. They were played to Fife the day after they were recorded, with Bates writing:

> You have now had an opportunity of hearing tapes of some of the extensive debriefing of Milligan undertaken by Bureau officers. In summary, Milligan has alleged that a group in Brisbane comprising senior police officers and an ex-police officer who are involved in illegal activities have extensive contacts in most areas of law enforcement through which they can manipulate or control investigative activities.*

Bates was obviously referring to Lewis, Murphy and Hallahan.

How much attention the content of Bates's memorandum and the Milligan Tapes were given by the Federal Government I do not know, but they were soon overshadowed by the arrival of another document. The day after Fife received Bates's warning, the Governor-General formally received the interim report of the Williams royal commission.

The memorandum from Bates had confirmed that the Bureau's integrity was under attack from corrupt police officers in Queensland. Seven years later, when Tony Fitzgerald would say that there were corrupt police in Queensland, Australia would believe him – but in 1979 nobody believed Milligan. Williams's interim report didn't

---

* Parliamentary Papers of Wal Fife, National Library of Australia, Canberra.

touch on corrupt police in Queensland; instead, it advised the government not to fight for the Bureau's integrity, and to get rid of the unit altogether.

10

The Record of Interview

WHILE THE BUREAU'S INTEGRITY was being questioned, Caswell and I were still preparing evidence for the Operation Jungle case. On 19 September, an opportunity to gather further evidence arose. I received a telephone call from Superintendent Hounslow of the Metropolitan Reception Centre at Long Bay Gaol, where Milligan was still in solitary confinement for his own protection.

Hounslow informed me that Milligan had sought his assistance in contacting me, and said that he could have Milligan in his office at 3.00 pm that afternoon in order for Milligan to speak with me on the telephone. When we spoke, Milligan stated he would like me to come to Sydney and interview him in relation to the Jane Table Mountain heroin drop. And so, on 24 September 1979, I flew to Sydney to sit down once again with Milligan.

The Milligan Tapes and the Milligan Record of

Interview were two very different scenarios. When conducting the formal interview, I was no longer free to let Milligan 'have his head' and talk about whatever he wanted, but instead needed to keep him focused on his role in the planning and implementation of the investigation that we both knew by the codename Operation Jungle.

Most people would expect, and rightly so, that someone who has been arrested is under a fair amount of pressure. But the arresting officer is under just as much stress. The arresting officer is responsible for bringing the whole investigation – which in our case represented fourteen months of work by three men – to a successful culmination. When I sat down with Milligan, I knew that the competency, or lack thereof, that I displayed during the interview would affect my career.

Any number of more senior officers, as well as members of the Crown Law Office, would be scrutinising my every word and every path that I went down in search of an admission by Milligan. And when the matter finally got to court, Milligan's defence counsel would come down hard on me, looking for the slightest crack in my evidence that they could, if only by bluff or bullshit, open into a fatal chasm. (I always thought it odd that while witnesses were obliged to tell the truth, no such obligation was placed upon counsel for the defence. In court, they were free to offer up the most outrageous allegations against me and my fellow agents as if they were statements of fact.)

I was reasonably well prepared to question Milligan. In addition to the false-bottomed suitcase evidence and the paper trail of receipts that we had discovered, the search of Milligan's room in Sutherland Street, Paddington, had provided bank receipts for transfers of money from Milligan to Hallahan.

However, I also knew that in this interview we would only be talking about Milligan himself, and not others whom he had no qualms about 'ratting on'. He wouldn't be allowed to ramble or jump from topic to topic; he would be under pressure to answer specific questions. Questions that would incriminate him. I wondered if his attitude towards me would change because of this. I decided to take it slowly and let him come to the realisation that confessing to me was the best option that he was going to get.

I knew that Milligan had initially been expecting to receive bail following his arrest, so I began by addressing this issue. 'Nobody's going to bail you out, John. Neither Hallahan nor any of his mates in the Queensland police have any influence over me. You've been arrested by the Federal Bureau of Narcotics, and they can't put any pressure on us.'

His expression confirmed that he understood what this meant.

'We've been investigating your involvement in the North Queensland heroin importation since January. We know all about the involvement of Bridge, Parker, Barron and Hallahan. We've got the receipt for your $26,000 bank transfer to Hallahan. We've been to Jane Table Mountain, and we've interviewed Dave Ward. We're thorough, John – we've spent almost twelve months exclusively investigating you. It doesn't matter to me if you don't want to say anything, but I would prefer it that the court hears your version of what happened, not mine.'

I had never believed in the 'need-to-know' theory, taught at many detective courses, that you shouldn't let the offender know what you have on them because that will assist their defence. On the contrary, I've found that when an investigation has been done thoroughly, when the suspect realises how much evidence has been gathered, there's every chance that there won't be a defence. Why drag out the inevitable? The ideal situation is that they tap the mat and plead guilty. The majority of offenders that I'd arrested had done just that.

I'd also never believed in the tactic of starting with flimsy evidence and 'beating it out of them', or 'verballing' or 'loading' them. (It had been known to happen, of course, with forces consisting of officers who were lazy, not too bright, or under pressure to produce a quick result.) I'd been trained to rely on sound investigative techniques to conclude investigations, and I worked for an organisation that appreciated that a thorough investigation took time – and was prepared to give us that time.

'John, I'll tell you what I can offer: the truth. When you front court, I'm not going to paint you out to be the worst villain that ever existed. I'm not going to tell the court that you were the mastermind of this importation. I believe you took orders from Glen Hallahan. I'm not going to verbal you, but I do already know a hell of a lot.'

Milligan looked up at me, and, with a sigh of resignation, he said, 'Yes, Mr Shobbrook, I realise that.'

At 4.45 pm on 24 September 1979, I commenced the formal typewritten Record of Interview with John Milligan in relation to Operation Jungle. Present during the interview as a witness was Ian Lloyd, who had transferred to the Narcotics Bureau.

Milligan's answers to my questions were detailed. At times, all I needed to say to keep his narrative flowing was, 'Go on,' or, 'What happened then?' Milligan did not hold back any details of the importation of the heroin into North Queensland, and named fourteen individuals who had played a part.

He told me that thoughts of importing drugs into North Queensland by light aircraft had been around long before he and Hallahan teamed up. 'A man I knew as Peter McGovern was a dealer in heroin, and had been party to bringing in some buddha sticks by light aircraft a few months before,' he stated. 'When I met Peter McGovern, he told me that he was in contact with a pilot who lived on the North Shore of Sydney, and that he, McGovern, was trying to raise capital to fly drugs into Australia. McGovern told me that he needed capital because he, McGovern, a man named Terry Haddaway, the pilot and a private detective from the Western Suburbs of Sydney, whose name I cannot accurately remember at the moment, but [it] was a name like Tarlington, had imported drugs – buddha sticks – by light aircraft just recently. The private detective had ripped them off. [McGovern] asked me if I knew anyone who could make enquiries into the activities of the private detective.'

I asked Milligan if he had approached Hallahan – if this

was where Hallahan first became aware of the possibilities of light aircraft drug importations.

'Within a couple of weeks, I was having a conversation about another matter with a man I feel unable to name at the moment,' Milligan continued. 'He asked me what was the truth of the story that Courtney [a drug courier friend] had apparently told him about a pilot wishing to fly drugs into Australia. In another discussion I had with this unnamed man and another associate, Bryan William Parker, the man asked me to discuss the matter further with McGovern.'

Milligan wouldn't name Hallahan in the Record of Interview, which he knew would end up in open court. I couldn't blame him; at that time, Hallahan had the taint of at least three murders hanging over his head – those of Raymond John Bailey, Jack Cooper and Shirley Brifman.

'McGovern introduced me to a man I now know as Ian Barron,' Milligan said. 'Barron told me that he was a highly qualified pilot and wished to smuggle drugs in if capital was provided. McGovern suggested smuggling the drugs from New Guinea as he had been told that other persons were already doing this.

'At a further discussion between the unnamed man, Parker and myself, the unnamed man agreed to finance a trip by Parker to Thailand to purchase heroin and indicated he would make sufficient funds for the trip available within one month.'

'Where did this meeting between you, Parker and the unnamed man take place?' I asked.

'Brisbane,' Milligan confirmed.

'Did you have any further meetings before these funds became available?'

'I met the unnamed man on two other occasions. On one occasion he handed me $1,000 in cash to give to Bryan Parker towards a trip to New Guinea with the pilot to acquaint himself with Civil Aviation requirements and airstrips in New Guinea and North Queensland. The unnamed man also suggested that he would underwrite expenses for Bryan Parker to book air tickets.'

At 6.25 pm, Milligan said to me, 'Look, Mr Shobbrook, I'm getting a bit tired and these incidents were a number of years ago. I'm sure I can remember them in the correct sequence if you give me some time to think about it.'

At 2.00 pm the following day, I recommenced my interview with Milligan. He started by telling me that at times he had Bridge and Parker confused as to who had done what, so he clarified the situation.

He then continued, 'I telephoned the unnamed person several times in this period to tell him what they were doing. I remember he told me not to get directly involved myself [...] I remember the unnamed person saying something to the effect [of], "It's just incredible that you can just walk off a plane at Port Moresby airport without any checks or anything." He inferred [sic] that he had this information from contacts in New Guinea; of [the] Administration he said, "They're just bloody hopeless."'

The interview then covered Milligan's and Parker's travel dates, and Milligan's documentation into and out of

New Guinea for the test flight, following which Milligan stated, 'I telephoned the unnamed man. I was excited and told him Parker had gone up to New Guinea and back secretly and it could be done.'

'What happened then?' I asked.

'I think I met the unnamed man shortly afterwards to collect some money from him. I just forget now, but it could have been to pay Barron a further fee for the flight.'

'Where did the discussion about the further flight originate from?' I asked.

'It had been discussed generally before with the unnamed man and it was definitely decided [by] the time I met him after Barron's first flight, because, just after, I met the unnamed man on a lonely road in a car and he provided me with several thousand dollars – I think it was $3,000 – towards Parker arranging a trip overseas as soon as possible. I know where this meeting took place but I cannot say in these circumstances as it may disclose the identity of the person.'

Milligan then detailed the trip by Parker to Bangkok to purchase the heroin, the use of the false-bottomed suitcase to fly it into New Guinea, and Barron's role in bringing the two parcels of heroin into North Queensland. He told me about his various attempts to recover the heroin, bringing Althaus, Kirkwood and Ward into the story.

Towards the end of the interview, Milligan said, 'Calculating the money transfers to the unnamed man […] it was between $15,000 and $25,000 that I knew about.'

In a manila folder labelled 'J. Milligan' sitting on the desk in front of Milligan was an original bank deposit transfer receipt for the sum of $26,000 paid into the account of Glen Hallahan at the King George Square, Brisbane branch of the Commonwealth Trading Bank. Yet Milligan still would not put in writing the name of the person who had financed the importation, and who on at least seventeen occasions had communicated with him by telephone and instructed him as the plan was put into effect. Such was Milligan's fear of Hallahan.

Following the formal interview, when I asked Milligan about the $26,000 he had deposited into Hallahan's bank account in Brisbane, he confirmed my belief that this money resulted from the sale, in Sydney, of the single parcel of heroin that had been recovered on Jane Table. Should they ever be questioned about the deposit, Milligan told me, he and Hallahan had hatched a plan to claim that the $26,000 was payment for the sale of a parcel of land adjoining Hallahan's home at Obi Obi.

11

Disbanded

WHILE I WAS INTERVIEWING Milligan and gathering strong evidence against Hallahan and those working above him, the Australian Royal Commission of Inquiry into Drugs was coming down hard on the Bureau of Narcotics.

For me, the alarm bells that the royal commission was targeting the Bureau had started to ring the first time I met Royal Commissioner Williams. During a demonstration by a Customs drug detection dog in my own office around September 1979, Williams had joked, 'I think one dog is just as productive as one Harvey Bates.' To make such a derogatory comment about the Director of the Federal Bureau of Narcotics – and in the presence of his staff – was hardly appropriate for a royal commissioner.

Williams hounded Bates from the start of the royal commission, making unfounded allegations that he and the Bureau were more interested in self-aggrandisement than drug law enforcement. Williams's arrogance towards our Bureau chief was exemplified when Bates was kept waiting for three days after travelling to Brisbane to give evidence to the commission because Williams, who also happened to be chairman of the Queensland Turf Club, had gone to the races.

In his interim report, submitted to Governor-General Sir Zelman Cowen on 18 September 1979, Williams left no room for doubt, writing 'THIS COMMISSION STRONGLY RECOMMENDS THAT THE NARCOTICS BUREAU BE DISBANDED.' Williams's justification for this recommendation included, among other items:

- Distrust of the Narcotics Bureau among other law enforcement bodies.
- Relationships between the Narcotics Bureau and state police are bad.
- Generally speaking, the Narcotics Bureau's reputation for efficiency is lower than that of state police forces.
- Notwithstanding some admirable initiatives, it has contributed to morale problems in other areas in the Bureau of Customs.
- The training of the Narcotics Bureau officers leaves much to be desired.
- Too much central control impairs the Bureau's operational efficiency.
- The Narcotics Bureau has traded upon a flattering image.
- Career opportunities for Narcotics Bureau officers are too restricted.

- The Narcotics Bureau has demonstrated itself overly secretive in its dealings with other agencies.
- Narcotics Bureau officers have in the main been recruited from Customs preventive officers but experience as preventive officers is an insufficient practical training for today's investigators of drug trafficking.

Notably, there was nothing in the interim report about ineptitude, corruption, incompetence or dishonesty. Williams's findings concerning the Bureau boiled down to the fact that the state police forces didn't like us, we kept secrets, we were overly controlled from Canberra and we were apparently a bunch of smart-arses.

When Williams expanded on his justification for recommending that the Bureau be disbanded, he raised three specific problems:

1. First, the Narcotics Bureau is founded on an insufficient legislative base.
2. Secondly, it has become apparent that persons who, by any standards, would be classified as criminals are now deeply engaged in the illegal trade in drugs.
3. Thirdly, the total staff of the Narcotics Bureau is far too small.

He pointed out that the Bureau operated under Sections 233a and 233b of the *Customs Act*, which specifically relate to offences involving prohibited imports – for the Bureau this meant prohibited drugs – and that this placed a restriction on the activities of the Narcotics Bureau should a criminal be engaged in other types of offences. Williams expressed misgivings that because the Narcotics Bureau was 'staffed by public servants', it was not up to dealing with intelligent and often dangerous criminals. He lamented that the Commonwealth police was the only Federal Police Force with an Australia-wide presence, yet they had been 'enjoined from enforcing the *Customs Act*'. Williams also pointed out that 'the Narcotics Bureau still does not number 200 persons yet it is endeavouring to fulfil a very large role'.

In reply to Williams's concerns, the Narcotics Bureau stated that the remedy for any deficiencies that it may have was to increase its powers, resources and staff. The Prime Minister had suggested a similar course of action in July 1979 when he asked Williams to look into the question of improvements relating to the Narcotics Bureau, yet Williams offered no such recommendations.

The interim report was the most appropriate means of supplying the government with proof that the Narcotics Bureau was inept and corrupt, and instead the document contained generalisations and opinion, and not one hard fact supporting ineptitude or corruption.

Tim Besley, the Permanent Head of Minister Wal Fife's department, wrote to Fife expressing his concerns: 'I find it hard to see how the Commission could come to the conclusion that it has. It has given no reasons – it is not an argued judgement as would be the case if it were a decision of the High Court.'

~

When on 22 October 1979 Harvey Bates became aware of the Williams commission's recommendation, he sent a briefing note to Minister Fife, referring to Milligan's arrest and expressing concern that there were people and organisations that would benefit from the destruction of the Bureau:

> Following a debrief of a person arrested for conspiracy offences involving heroin importations I had reason to again bring this view to your attention. On this occasion I outlined some of the motives which were possibly behind the attack against the Federal Narcotics Bureau and nominated the Royal Commission of Inquiry into Drugs as one of the forums being used (albeit unwittingly) for these purposes.
>
> It is my view that if the fundamental recommendation in this Interim Report [...] is accepted and acted upon by the Government, the objectives of certain persons and organisations as outlined in my previous minute to you will be achieved, ultimately with disastrous consequences for the Australian public and the regional enforcement effort against drug trafficking. For this reason I consider it essential that the foregoing comments and the additional facts detailed hereunder are made known to the Government before any decision is taken on the full range of the recommendations contained in the Interim Report.

Whether Harvey Bates was serious or being politically correct when he said that the royal commission of inquiry into drugs was 'unwittingly' being used to attack the Bureau I do not know, but there was nothing unwitting about Williams's attacks – they were intentional. Fife acted on Bates's report, and on 1 November wrote to Prime Minister Fraser, saying:

> Mr Bates, Commissioner of the Federal Bureau of Narcotics, has given me a report dated 22-10-79 in which he comments on what he sees as a concerted effort to denigrate the Federal Narcotics Bureau.
>
> In that document Mr Bates also referred to the arrest of John Edward Milligan who indicated at the time of his arrest that he was prepared to co-operate with the Bureau by providing information on drug trafficking.
>
> Mr Bates reported that Milligan appeared to be in possession of knowledge which suggested that senior officers of the Queensland Police Force were involved in criminal activity.
>
> So far as the allegations relating to a former officer and serving members of the Queensland Police Force were concerned, it was decided that investigations would continue to the point where the allegations were either disproved or where there was sufficient hard evidence to report the matter to Queensland authorities.
>
> The documents I have referred to in this letter raise serious matters which I consider ought to be brought to your attention in relation to consideration of the Interim Report from the Australian Royal Commission of Inquiry into Drugs.

Fife was advising the Prime Minister not to act too quickly on Williams's recommendation to disband the Bureau, for to do so would end the Narcotics Bureau's investigations into the involvement in heroin trafficking by former and serving Queensland police officers.

On 2 November, the Department of the Prime Minister and Cabinet sent a briefing note to Fife in anticipation of a Cabinet meeting set for 5 November. The note stated:

> Why make the decision now? The Narcotics Bureau has been subjected to unfair media publicity, perhaps orchestrated by some circles to promote a climate for change.
>
> There are no details available as yet as to how the AFP would manage the narcotics function. Such details should be available to complete the picture for the consideration of the Government.
>
> The Milligan tapes, details of which have been made available to the Prime Minister, need assessment and action in terms of enforcement connections.
>
> It is important to note that the interim report makes no statement about corruption in the Narcotics Bureau.

Minister Fife had reasoned that the right time to decide upon the future of the Bureau was once the final report of the royal commission was released, which was expected on or around 12 November. A Cabinet meeting was due to be held the following day, which would be the appropriate time and place to discuss this important matter.

As it transpired, there was no Cabinet discussion on 13 November concerning the rights or wrongs of Williams's recommendation to disband the Bureau. On the afternoon of 6 November 1979, with the dust from the Melbourne Cup horse race still hanging in the air, the Deputy Prime Minister, Doug Anthony, rose in parliament to speak.

'The Royal Commission identified three main factors in support of its recommendation [to disband the Narcotics Bureau],' he said. 'In brief they are: 1. the Narcotics Bureau is founded on an insufficient legislative base; 2. persons who by any standards would be classified as criminals are deeply engaged in the illegal trade in drugs; 3. the total staff of the Narcotics Bureau is too small.

'The Narcotics Bureau claims that the simple remedy for any deficiencies it may have is to increase its staff, powers and resources. The [Williams Royal] Commission rejects this cure, which, in its opinion, would compound the problem, not solve it. The solution is to attach the main functions of the Narcotics Bureau to the Australian Federal Police.'

The Opposition Leader, Labor's Bill Hayden, a former Queensland police officer, then chose to sink his boot in. 'There is evidence of corruption,' he claimed. 'The Queensland Police Force, among other law-enforcement agencies, has said that. For the last two and a half years it has been a frequent complaint by law-enforcement officers in state police forces that the Bureau has been heavily infected with corruption.'

However, there was no evidence of this apparent

'corruption'. Royal Commissioner Williams's interim report had not made a single reference to finding corruption within the Narcotics Bureau, but now the leader of the federal opposition was claiming in parliament that state police officers had known of our corruption 'for the last two and a half years'. It was absurd.

Even as these significant events unfolded, Operation Jungle continued. On 31 October 1979, Caswell and I were once again back in Sydney. We were driving to Fairfield, in the western suburbs of Sydney, to visit the head office of the local operations of Japanese electronics manufacturer Sharp.

The production of my Narcotics Bureau identification brought a concerned general manager to the front office. He took us into his office, where his face went ashen when I told him that I was about to arrest his Service Manager, Ian Barron. The general manager's main concern wasn't for Barron, I soon realised, but for the adverse publicity that the company might receive because of his man's criminal behaviour.

'Call Barron to your office and we'll deal with it discreetly,' I said. 'And ask him to bring his coat – he won't be coming back for a while.'

Some people become anxious when they are arrested; others get abusive. Milligan had been rather nonplussed, but when Barron appeared, his reaction staggered me – he was excited. It was as if we'd told him that we were from the lottery office and he had the winning ticket. He couldn't wait to get into our car.

'Where are we going?' he asked.

'We'll just drop by our office, where we can have a chat without any interruptions,' I replied.

It was more than an hour's drive from Sydney's western suburbs to Customs House at Circular Quay, but Barron didn't mind. The arrest seemed to give him a buzz. He was delighting in his newfound notoriety and the attention we were giving him.

Barron was interviewed in the same room at Customs House in which I had interviewed Milligan some weeks earlier. He was charged with a breach of Section 86(1)(a) of the *Commonwealth Crimes Act*, in conjunction with Section 233B(1)(b) of the *Customs Act*, concerning a conspiracy to import a quantity of heroin into Australia between January and October 1977. At his court appearance he pleaded guilty to the charges brought against him.

The following week, on 5 November, Caswell and I drove from Brisbane to Grafton, in northern New South Wales, to interview and arrest Graham Bridge for his role in the heroin importations. Bridge declined to participate in a formal record of interview, but made a number of verbal admissions following his arrest. Bridge would also plead guilty to the charges when he was brought to court.

Our next target for arrest was the apparent leader of the syndicate: Glen Hallahan.

On Melbourne Cup day, Noel and I were driving back to Brisbane. We were staggered to hear an announcement on our car radio that the Federal Bureau of Narcotics was to soon be disbanded. I was the Acting Regional Commander for the Northern Region at that time, and the following morning I flew to Canberra to be briefed.

While I was in Canberra, my Operation Jungle colleague John Moller decided to speak out. Using the name 'Paul', he telephoned a talkback program on Brisbane radio station 4IP and made allegations of official and police corruption in Queensland. His comments would be printed in *The Courier-Mail* on 8 November under the headline 'Politicians Linked to Drug Raids'. The Queensland Police Force and the Queensland Government were not pleased.

Now that the Narcotics Bureau was to be wound up, on 14 November 1979 I was temporarily sworn in to the Australian Federal Police (AFP) as a 'Special Member' by Superintendent R.H. (Bob) Gillespie.

An 'offer of appointment' didn't automatically amount to a permanent police position in the AFP, however. The AFP's first commissioner, Sir Colin Woods, qualified the situation to *The Canberra Times* on 11 December 1979:

Those former agents will discover that their lot has been greatly improved in terms of career prospects. It would, however, be unrealistic of me not to acknowledge publicly that the transition of some former narcotics agents to police ranks presents a complex set of problems for the police [...] I have told them that as potential police officers, they must of course be acceptable not only to me, but to my police colleagues in the States.

I realised it was unlikely that I, as a former narcotics agent who had sought to imprison Glen Hallahan, would receive the seal of approval from Hallahan's fellow state police colleagues and Rat Packers Terry Lewis and Tony Murphy.

12

The Public Hearings

THE WILLIAMS ROYAL COMMISSION was due to conclude on 21 December 1979, when Williams wrote to Governor-General Sir Zelman Cowen, saying, 'I have the honour to present to you the Report of the Australian Royal Commission of Inquiry into Drugs.' However, as 1980 dawned, the commission's public hearings continued.

The commission was extended because of the comments Moller had made on Brisbane talkback radio. Although the Queensland Government was decidedly unhappy, the premier, Joh Bjelke-Petersen, was forced on 21 November 1979 to ask Justice Williams to extend his royal commission and look into these corruption allegations.

Williams did so, and consequently asked the Narcotics Bureau for copies of all intelligence that adversely named current or former Queensland police officers or politicians. This placed before Williams, and his Queensland police investigators, the complete Operation Jungle investigation, the evidence of Hallahan's involvement and the confidential Milligan Tapes.

On 3 January I was called to appear before the commission as a witness. It would be the first of five such visits. I had never appeared before a royal commission, but I had considerable experience as a witness in both district and supreme courts. I imagined that this would be similar, with an impartial judge and the counsel assisting being less severe than the usual defence counsel. How wrong I was. From the start, Commissioner Williams and his Counsel Assisting, Cedric Hampson QC, displayed considerable hostility towards me.

I wondered what had prompted this. They had no doubt read the Operation Jungle dossier, and listened to the Milligan Tapes. There was nothing in either source of which I was ashamed, or that I wished to hide.

In a short space of time, both Williams and Hampson were accusing me of fabricating Milligan's claims against Hallahan in order to harm the Queensland Police Force and make the Federal Bureau of Narcotics look good by comparison. I acknowledge that this was a potential side-effect of Operation Jungle, as Hallahan was clearly involved and Lewis and Murphy had been mentioned, but that hadn't been our objective.

Hampson attacked me over the tapes. 'There are gaps in tape recordings, aren't there – places where you stopped the tape?'

'Yes,' I replied.

'I put it to you that the reason you stopped the tape was for you to suggest these things to Milligan.'

'That's not true at all,' I said in return. 'The breaks in the tape were at Milligan's request when he wanted to mention something that he didn't want recorded.'

'In effect, you led Milligan on until he gave you what you wanted.'

'I encouraged him to keep on talking,' I said, 'but I didn't put words in his mouth.'

'You mentioned Lickiss to him, didn't you?'

Bill Lickiss was a Liberal politician who, on 10 March 1975, had been appointed to the Queensland Cabinet as Minister for Survey, Valuation, Urban and Regional Affairs, with a further promotion to Attorney-General and Minister for Justice on 13 August 1976 under Premier Joh Bjelke-Petersen.

'No,' I said, but Hampson didn't appear to be grasping what I was saying.

'You put Milligan up to it, in the sense of raising it first, you know, perhaps off the record or so.'

'That's not what happened,' I said.

'It is quite clear you brought Lickiss's name up; there is no doubt about that.'

Based on what? I wondered. Hampson was making assumptions and putting them forward as irrefutable fact.

'That's not true,' I said. 'That's not how our conversation took place.'

'Where else would Milligan have got it from?'

'You would have to ask Milligan that.'

'Milligan would not have mentioned Lickiss unless somebody had directed his attention to him.'

Milligan had mentioned dozens upon dozens of people

on the tapes – was Hampson seriously suggesting that I had directed his attention to each and every name? For me, there was nothing outstanding about Lickiss anyway.

'It wasn't me,' I said.

'This is what you said: "Anyway, I know that Lickiss is crook and Scullion knows that Lickiss is into drug trafficking."'

Hampson had the Milligan Tapes and the printed transcripts, but the words he was quoting were not recorded on the transcripts. He knew that he couldn't confront me with proof of these lies because that proof didn't exist. I never said that.

'You should listen to Scullion's master tapes,' I said. 'They contain the "off the record" pauses and you'll know that we didn't put Milligan up to anything or suggest anything to him.'

'The problem is,' Hampson went on, 'that he [Milligan] has very seriously told you one story and very seriously told the Commission investigator a completely opposite story. It is the old question: how do we know to whom he was telling the truth, or on either occasion telling the truth?'

I couldn't figure out what I was missing. Had the royal commission previously discovered overwhelming wrongdoing by the Narcotics Bureau that I was unaware of? And was I being tarred with the same brush?

I tried again and again to explain why the tapes had been paused during the interview. Hampson simply ignored anything I said, and hammered away with his theory that I had put Milligan up to it. Hampson then accused me of being 'a bit naive' – and I was! I still held to the belief that the truth would surface. I was sure I would emerge from Hampson's badgering unscathed, because I was telling the truth. And I believed that when I left the witness box I would get back to work, complete the Hallahan brief of evidence, arrest him, extradite him to New South Wales and place him in front of a judge. I had an above-board brief of evidence, I told myself. The Bureau mightn't exist, but I still had the power of arrest. When I got out of the commission hearing, I'd arrest Hallahan and wipe the smirk off Williams's face, and deflate the puffed-up Hampson. Any respect I had held for this royal commission was fast evaporating.

Following Hampson's unfounded accusations, the Honourable Justice Edward Williams glared at me from his elevated position in the court, pointed a finger and said with considerable gravitas, 'If I can prove that you have perjured yourself before this commission, then you will be going to jail.'

The shock I felt was as though a doctor had just told me I had a terminal illness. In front of a packed courtroom, a bar table full of lawyers and a throng of journalists, I had just been threatened with imprisonment. My mind was racing – something was very wrong in that courtroom. I knew I hadn't committed perjury, but Hampson had been 'massaging' the facts, and he and Williams had all the power. I was starting to feel like a lamb to the slaughter. What would these bastards be prepared to do to sink me?

Later that same day, Milligan was called for the first time as a witness before the commission. I was in the public gallery as Milligan entered the witness box. Having gone through the formality of swearing to tell the truth, he asked if he could make an application to the court; Milligan clearly hadn't forgotten the formalities of his old days as a judge's associate.

Williams invited Milligan to go ahead and make his application.

'Your Honour, I am prepared to cooperate with your royal commission,' Milligan said. 'My application to the commission is simply to be permitted to give my evidence in camera.' Milligan, who would be heading back to jail after giving his evidence, did not want to be an informant – a 'dog' – in open court and with the media in attendance.

Williams swiftly dismissed Milligan's request. 'There has been too much said to this commission off the record; if you have any allegations to make then you'll make them in public.'

In all, the commission would permit 603 witnesses to give their evidence in camera, yet it refused to take confidential evidence from Milligan. I knew enough about court procedures to know that Williams should not be discouraging a witness from giving evidence – no matter in what format.

Later, when it suited the commission's need to conceal evidence, it would keep a written statement by Milligan – a statement that implicated Hallahan – hidden from the public and the media.

Williams, in justifying his decision to deny Milligan confidentiality, wrote in his final report:

During his evidence on these matters, Milligan suggested that he should continue in an in-camera session. This posed difficulty to the Commission; for if Milligan intended to incriminate Shobbrook it was only fair that Shobbrook should hear what was said.

Fairness to me! This was a first for the Williams royal commission. At no time had Milligan ever indicated that he 'intended to incriminate' me. But Williams and Hampson undoubtedly hoped that he would, especially with a little encouragement from them. As it transpired, Milligan would take a courageous stance and defend me against Hampson's persistent efforts to discredit me.

Having already been sentenced, Milligan had nothing to gain by talking candidly to the royal commission. Indeed, he could lose his life if he stood in a public courtroom, with the media present, and detailed his knowledge of Hallahan's and others' corruption in the state of Queensland. Hallahan had some nasty mates in the New South Wales Police Force, and there were no doubt crims in Long Bay Gaol who would like to be in those coppers' good books.

Consequently, Williams and Hampson's strategy worked. Milligan maintained from the witness box that he knew of no wrongdoing by Hallahan in relation to drug matters. He wouldn't name anyone in open court, but, to his credit, neither would he allow Williams and Hampson to 'verbal' him into alleging that I was corrupt.

Hampson needed Milligan to confirm statements that Milligan had made to the royal commission's investigators, Ray Phillips and Barrie O'Brien. Hampson recounted Milligan's interview with the two men, saying, 'You said, "Shobbrook had put me in a state of fear, and he put a proposition to me that if I could come up with a good story before Scullion arrived to tell Scullion that he would assist me in many ways which he named" – is that true?'

'I told Phillips and O'Brien that, yes,' Milligan acknowledged.

Hampson, believing he had found a way to discredit my evidence, emphasised the point by raising his voice and repeating his question. 'Is that true?'

Then Milligan burst Hampson's bubble. 'Not entirely true.'

Hampson's face turned red. Raising his voice, he became insistent. 'He made a suggestion […] that if you could come up with a good story before Scullion arrived?'

I had one champion in that courtroom – John Milligan, who calmly countered Hampson's melodramatic bombast. 'It is unfair to Shobbrook to say anything that infers [sic] that we concocted a story, or he was concocting a story,' he told the royal commission. 'He believed that what he was doing was in the best interests of the Bureau, and was honest. So it is untrue to say that, to say that he wanted me to come up with a good story, but he wanted as much information as I could give him.'

Hampson's badgering continued. He described the tapes as 'a ridiculous conversation' with 'ill-based assumptions'.

Milligan would not agree with Hampson's scenario. 'No, it wasn't anything like that at all. I gave him what I had been told from a number of sources [...] I did not invent things.'

Royal commission investigator O'Brien, when interviewing Milligan, had put to him, 'You are saying he [Shobbrook] suggested certain things to you off the tape, turned the tape on and then you repeated it as though it was information that you had first-hand?'

Hampson now questioned Milligan about this, and Milligan answered, 'Yes, I said that to O'Brien but that's not—' Hampson then cut Milligan off, not allowing him to complete his answer. But, after two further questions, Milligan completed the answer that Hampson had tried to keep from entering the record. 'But I want to say the way the context of that first part of what you read reads as if Shobbrook put the words in my mouth to say on tape, but that is not the way it was done. That is not true.'

Hampson would not relent in his efforts to have one scenario prevail: the idea that I had corruptly concocted stories concerning illegal activities by various persons and fed them to Milligan, and that Milligan had then simply regurgitated them for the tape recorder. Hampson would not concede that there was any other possibility – that the events had unfolded just as Milligan had stated, for instance, and that they had been confirmed by documentation that the Narcotics Bureau had supplied to the royal commission, as well as by the brief of evidence we were developing against Hallahan.

When Milligan's evidence ended for the day on 3 January, Commissioner Williams suggested that he be given copies of the transcripts of his record of interview with Phillips and O'Brien in order to 'refresh his memory' overnight. This was the interview in which Milligan had said that I had 'suggested certain things' to him – words that he had now told the commission were 'not entirely true'. Clearly, Williams wanted Milligan to repeat this version of events when he continued giving evidence the next day.

The following morning, Hampson recommended questioning Milligan. 'You took a copy of that exhibit [the transcripts] overnight. I would like to direct you back to what we were talking about when the commission adjourned yesterday afternoon and ask you what is correct: the account you gave Mr Shobbrook or the account that you gave to Mr Phillips and Mr O'Brien, or is there some intermediate account?'

'The account that I gave Mr Shobbrook is correct,' Milligan stated. 'Where there is variation with the account I gave Mr Phillips and Mr O'Brien, I think the Shobbrook account is correct.'

The commission's plan hadn't worked; Milligan was sticking to his guns and refusing to take the opportunity offered by Hampson – with a transcript supplied by Williams – to sink me.

Hampson quickly changed the subject. 'You are not saying he [Hallahan] ever had anything to do with drugs, are you?'

'Well, I don't wish to answer that question,' was all Milligan would say. He was refusing to deliver the 'no' that Hampson was hoping for.

Hampson kept trying. 'You apparently told Phillips and O'Brien you had nothing at all to connect Hallahan with drugs.'

'Did I tell them that?' came Milligan's reply, which almost reduced the courtroom to laughter.

Hampson then spoke at length. 'He [Shobbrook] thought that you knew a lot more than in fact you did. He thought that you were a real big wheel. And you are not. He was sitting there open-mouthed waiting for this big man to tell him everything, and you did not have much to tell him. So you put forward hearsay – rumour – speculation, and you were quick, I suggest, to offer him anything at all, even though it would have been hearsay eight times removed, to confirm or to assist him in obtaining any confirmation of the matters that he put to you. Shobbrook was a bit naive.'

Was I naive? The Woodward Royal Commission into Drug Trafficking certainly wouldn't have agreed. In October 1979, it had delivered its final report to the New South Wales Government, in which it had found Milligan to be a major figure in the importation of heroin into Australia. Indeed, an entire chapter of Royal Commissioner Woodward's report had been devoted to 'the Milligan Group', and Woodward had stated:

I do not accept that Milligan played only a minor role in this activity; merely carrying out the instructions of others. Rather, I regard him as the instigator and principal of much of this activity. I do not believe that I have been able to uncover all of that in which he has been involved. But even the limited amount of activity dealt with by me discloses a pattern of continual and persistent drug importation and trafficking activity over the years.

Most police witnesses at court don't require defence counsel, as they aren't being accused of any crime. There was nobody in the royal commission's courtroom to 'look after my interests', as they say, by countering the false claims Hampson was making as he questioned Milligan and me. When I finally returned to the Narcotics Bureau office that afternoon – still a free man – I immediately telephoned Central Office and spoke to a senior officer.

He knew of the investigation and of my royal commission court appearance. I told him I was concerned about Williams's and Hampson's hostile and unjustified attacks on me, and about Williams's threat to jail me. I could use a legal representative in court, I said, to counter Hampson's attacks, but I also needed support from Central Office, which held copies of the Milligan Tapes, to prove that the stated content of my interviews and tape recordings with Milligan was genuine and not fabricated.

'John, you got yourself into this,' he replied. 'You can get yourself out.'

I couldn't believe this response. How had I got myself into this? I'd been carrying out my duties as an investigator for the Federal Bureau of Narcotics, and now as a witness before the royal commission. This senior officer knew the truth of the situation: he had been following this investigation for more than a year and had actively played a part – he'd 'got into this' with me.

To say that his reaction disappointed me greatly would be an understatement. Until that moment, I'd had more than a degree of respect for him. The AFP's version of the Narcotics Bureau had just cast me adrift, and it dawned on me that this senior officer wasn't going to take any action that might jeopardise his hopes of rising through the ranks of the newly formed AFP.

More a politician than a police officer, the same officer later shared his thoughts on arresting corrupt police officers with me. 'Why bother?' he said. 'As soon as you lock up one crook copper, two more pop up in his place.'

13

Just Two Simple Farmers

GLEN HALLAHAN APPEARED BEFORE the Williams royal commission on 5 February 1980, and again on 6 March 1980. He admitted that he had met Milligan on about six occasions at the Kangaroo Point Travelodge, but claimed that the purpose of these meetings was to discuss a plan for the two men to become partners in a project to grow sweet corn at Hallahan's property in Obi Obi. It would not have taken much questioning by Hampson to show that this was an implausible cover story, but there is no record that the royal commission asked Hallahan to show the product of those six meetings that were supposedly about growing sweet corn. Were any notes taken at those meetings? Did Hallahan or Milligan have any documentation about their farming efforts? And why wasn't Milligan questioned by Williams or Hampson about those meetings and Hallahan's claims?

When asked about the receipt found by Supervising Narcotics Agent Phil Lawrence and me in Milligan's room at Paddington, which showed that Milligan had deposited $26,000 into Hallahan's bank account, the timing of which coincided with the recovery of the parcel of heroin in North Queensland, Hallahan replied, 'That was for a small section of my property that I sold to Milligan. I left it to him to take care of the paperwork.'

'Have you got separate title to the land yet?' Hampson asked.

'No,' Hallahan replied.

Commissioner Williams accepted Hallahan's testimony concerning the supposed land sale, but I knew differently. After Milligan told me about the land-sale cover story in our interview, I had gone to the Queensland Land Titles Office and confirmed that no documentation existed for any land sale on Hallahan's property. Why didn't the royal commission investigators do the same?

Then there was the oddity of an allegedly honest former police officer doing business with someone with Milligan's criminal history. Why would Hallahan have no misgivings about selling land to an active drug trafficker and a man who had been convicted for using his premises for prostitution? Would any honest ex-police officer really be happy to have Milligan living next door to his wife and children, and would his wife and children encourage him to form a business partnership with a known drug trafficker and pimp?

Astoundingly, Hallahan claimed that he had no knowledge that Milligan was a drug trafficker, or of Milligan's convictions for possessing heroin and using his premises for prostitution. Hallahan had spent some twenty years in the Queensland Police Force, and in particular in the Consorting Squad, which specialised in tracking the movements of known criminals. Hallahan insisted that all his contacts with Milligan had been legitimate business dealings, and the royal commission accepted these absurd statements.

Hampson, in mock amazement and sympathy, shook his head and asked Hallahan, 'Why would Milligan fabricate stories about you?'

'That question has troubled me,' Hallahan replied, giving every impression of being the second half of a double act. 'But to my mind it would appear to me that the Narcotics Bureau – they have been anxious to prove some sort of corruption in the Queensland Police Force for some reason or other.'

Hampson added, 'On a promise of more lenient treatment, if the Narcotics Bureau agent who arrested him would tell the judge he cooperated with their investigation?'

'Exactly! Something like that,' a smiling Hallahan agreed.

I shook my head in disbelief. Now Hampson was providing Hallahan with answers. Whatever happened to 'don't coach the witness'?

Hampson pushed Hallahan further. 'And therefore Milligan would say things on tape that he believed the narcotics interrogator wanted to hear?'

'Yes,' confirmed Hallahan, snatching the 'get out of jail' card in the form of the guilt-free statements Hampson was offering.

I was in the court the day that Hallahan gave this evidence to the royal commission. It was the first time I had seen him in person. Tall, well-built and handsome, the man oozed charisma. With his smile and confidence, he looked like someone who couldn't help but be successful. But he had one serious flaw: greed. His face was familiar to me from several black-and-white photographs in the Operation Jungle files, but even better known to me was his reputation – not as the 'ace detective' who appeared in a photograph on a front-page *Sunday Truth* newspaper story titled 'Marihuana Seized in Swoop by Police on Weirdos', but as a sinister, callous criminal and potential killer.

As I watched Hallahan getting the 'kid glove treatment' in the witness box, I realised that I was a casualty in a deep, dark world of corruption. I had always understood law enforcement to be simple: the honest cop arrests the dishonest criminal. If the cop does his job correctly and thoroughly, the criminal goes to jail. Now everything around me was changing, and it seemed that being honest and doing your job thoroughly didn't matter. It was as if there was some secret society that I had blundered into, a society whose rules I didn't know and that I didn't want to join anyway – but everyone else was living by its rules.

The Williams royal commission occurred seven years before the Fitzgerald inquiry. Few people would believe that the highest levels of the police could possibly be corrupt, and fewer still would accept that a supreme court judge and a senior Queen's Counsel could be engaged in protecting a corrupt ex-police officer.

I felt deflated and isolated. This was wrong. A court shouldn't be twisting some facts and ignoring others. *I'll show the bastards*, I told myself. *They can say what they like here, but when this is over, I'll quietly arrest Hallahan and have him extradited to an honest court in New South Wales.* That thought sustained me.

I had prepared many briefs of evidence before, and I knew the one I had prepared against Hallahan was better than most. Proof of his guilt already existed in a safe in my office, so I felt confident of a conviction. Not for one moment did I suspect that the members of the secret society would stop me – not only by destroying my evidence, but by destroying me as well.

On 20 February 1980, two senior officers from Canberra flew to Brisbane to 'have a word' with me. At the close of business, once the other staff had left the office, they advised me that I should put an end to all the pressure and consider looking for work outside the AFP, in which I was still only a 'special member' and not a sworn-in permanent officer, possibly even return to the Customs department.

I was told that, should I choose to remain in the AFP, I would be unpopular, and could be denied promotion and restricted in my future duties. The more softly spoken of the two officers took the 'good cop' role, offering me friendly advice. The other officer was the 'bad cop', pointing out the harsh reality of the situation as he saw it.

The 'good cop', who knew that I liked dinghy sailing, said that I could be pensioned out of the force, buy a yacht and enjoy life. He said how he wished he had an opportunity like that. 'Forget about all of this and enjoy an early retirement with Jan,' he told me, like he was an old friend. Retirement? I was only thirty-one!

The 'bad cop' had also spoken to me as a friend in the past, but now his 'advice' was bordering on becoming threatening. He advised me to 'move interstate or be buried'. I think by this he meant that I would be buried somewhere in the Stores Branch, where I would spend the remainder of my career counting biros and paperclips.

'The Australian Federal Police Force don't need crusading investigators,' he told me bluntly. He advised me to voluntarily terminate Operation Jungle and cease my investigations into Hallahan's activities.

I told the officers that I intended to continue with my investigation, which had thus far led to the arrests of and guilty pleas from Milligan, Barron and Bridge. I saw no reason to terminate my enquiries into Hallahan's involvement, especially as the Deputy Crown Solicitor's Office in Brisbane had already told me that I had a *prima facie* case against him.

The officers shook their heads, gave me a look of disgust and left.

During telephone conversations over the following days, the 'bad cop' put a number of suggestions to me. Should I choose to voluntarily terminate Operation Jungle, he said it was possible that a narcotics 'liaison' position in Fiji could be arranged for me to fill. Or perhaps I would prefer a transfer to another state?

I explained that I had returned to Brisbane from Sydney to care for my elderly mother, and that I wouldn't abandon her for any transfer. One thing that the officer never offered was a promotion: I was enough trouble as a substantive Supervising Narcotics Agent (Inspector) – imagine the trouble that I might cause if I were a Chief Narcotics Agent (Regional Commander).

The officer explained that should I proceed to the stage of arresting Hallahan – and whomever else his arrest might lead to – then that would cause serious problems for the AFP. Hallahan's arrest would embarrass the Queensland Police Force, and, in retaliation, the police in Queensland could very well cease to provide the AFP and other Commonwealth authorities with the various forms of assistance that the AFP needed in order to perform its functions in Queensland. Those forms of assistance included various forensic and technical services, fingerprint examination, document examination, access to *modus operandi* records, and possibly even a refusal to lodge detained federal prisoners at local police stations during arrest situations. The AFP in Queensland, as in New South Wales, didn't have its own cells to lodge prisoners – we used the state police force's cells.

Following the calls from the officers in Canberra, Supervising Narcotics Agent Stephen Polden from the Sydney Bureau office got in contact with me. Polden was a long-time friend of mine and also a former Customs officer; we had attended the Victoria Police Detective Training School together in 1970. He knew that I was honest, and he was aware of the pressure that I was being placed under, not only by the Williams royal commission, but also by my senior Narcotics Bureau/AFP officers.

Polden warned me – as a friend; this was not a threat – that if I did not 'go quietly', they could get rid of me by 'setting me up'. He suggested that it would take no effort at all for a locker search to be carried out at the Brisbane Bureau office, and for a small parcel of heroin to be 'found' in my locker. A charge of possession of heroin would not only rid the AFP of me, but it would also be welcomed by Williams, Hampson and those Queensland Police Force officers who were attempting to prove that I was a corrupt officer who had fabricated evidence against innocent Queensland police officers, Hallahan in particular. And even if I was acquitted, fighting a trumped-up charge of possession of heroin would ruin me and my family financially.

14

The Werin Street Incident

As the Williams royal commission continued, I was also questioned on matters that did not relate to Milligan. Commissioner Williams took a specific interest in and badgered me over one matter in particular that Milligan had apparently mentioned in passing on the Milligan Tapes, but of which I had no independent knowledge. This matter would become known as the 'Werin Street Incident'.

It started with a letter that Williams had passed on to both Queensland Police Superintendent Tony Murphy and the Narcotics Bureau's regional commander at the time. The anonymous letter-writer alleged that there were 'enormous quantities' of drugs at a house in Werin Street, Tewantin, on the Sunshine Coast, 8 kilometres west of the coastal resort of Noosa. The Narcotics Bureau apparently looked into these claims and concluded that there was no evidence of any imported drugs being involved. The possession, sale and use of locally grown or manufactured drugs was the responsibility of the Queensland police's Drug Squad, so the Bureau left it for the state police to act upon the information.

The Bureau's decision not to become involved, though, was seized upon by Williams as a prime example of its ineptitude, and I became the target for his aggressive attack while seated in the witness box.

'Why didn't you act on this information?' Williams challenged me.

'Sir, at the time I didn't know anything about Werin Street,' I replied.

'Don't give me that – you were supposed to be second in charge of the office, weren't you?'

'I was second in charge, yes.'

'Then how could you not know about what was going on in your own office? I don't accept that you knew nothing about it.'

'I was involved in Operation Jungle.'

'You weren't working in a vacuum. It wasn't a big office – there was only about a dozen of you. You talked to your colleagues; how could you not know what they were doing? You didn't go around with your eyes closed, did you? Did you tell John Milligan about Werin Street?'

'No, I couldn't have – I knew nothing about it, and I still don't.' I was genuinely confused as to why I was being asked about this.

'Then why does Milligan mention Werin Street on your tapes? Are you claiming that you didn't tell him about it?'

'Milligan spoke for two days and mentioned a lot of

people and incidents. I can't recall anything of note about a Werin Street.'

'If you didn't tell Milligan, then who did?'

'I don't know,' I acknowledged. 'Maybe Glen Hallahan told him.'

'Humph!' was Williams's scornful dismissal of me.

I was alleged to have fed Milligan this information during the Milligan Tapes sessions, recorded on 12 and 13 September 1979, but that made no sense as I only learnt about the allegations around Werin Street from Justice Williams when I was in his witness box from January 1980. I had no idea who had told Milligan about Werin Street, but it certainly wasn't me.

In any case, I couldn't understand why an unimportant raid on a small suburban house was such a big issue. But Commissioner Williams's point seemed to be that I had participated in this raid and that something bad had happened. It wasn't until years later that I discovered that Williams wasn't being critical of how I'd conducted a raid at Werin Street; he was making a big deal out of the fact that I, or the Narcotics Bureau at least, had *not* participated in the raid on Werin Street.

I wasn't aware at the time that the Bureau had apparently left it to the Drug Squad to investigate the matter – that decision had been made by the regional commander without consulting me. And why should he have consulted me? Part of the understanding with Operation Jungle was that we were not to be interrupted by more minor operational matters, and a raid on a house based on an anonymous letter was as minor as they came.

It took years for the shocking truth of the Werin Street Incident to emerge, and it took a courageous Queensland police officer to reveal it. Detective Jim Slade, who had rejected bribes from his corrupt colleagues and in retaliation had been subjected to threats and physical intimidation, was an honest undercover officer. At the time of the Werin Street Incident, he worked under Superintendent Tony Murphy at the Bureau of Criminal Intelligence. Slade not only knew of the Werin Street raid, he was involved in it, and he made this public in 2014 in Matthew Condon's book *Jacks and Jokers*.

Slade described to Condon how Murphy ordered him to conduct surveillance on the house because 'the word was that there were enormous quantities of drugs on the premises'. Slade said that he carried out surveillance on the house for several weeks and came to the conclusion that the massive amounts of trafficking going on and drugs on the premises appeared to be exaggerated. As Slade said to Condon, 'Justice Williams told Tony Murphy to do a big thing on it and that he would use that as part of [his exposé of the] inadequacies and inefficiencies of the Narcotics Bureau.'

Murphy's hand-picked team of Queensland police officers had raided the premises and come out with an impressive quantity of drugs. They didn't have to spend much time searching the premises, for they had taken the drugs in with them.

As Slade explained, 'Tony [Murphy] knew about it prior to the letter coming in […] I don't know where this letter came from, whether it was sent in from the public or whether it was a letter generated by Tony Murphy, or generated by Justice Williams […] They took in the most incredible amount of drugs and busted these people, the whole thing was bullshit. Acting on that, Justice Williams recommended that the Narcotics Bureau be disbanded. That whole thing was worked out between Williams and Murphy.'

When Slade's allegations were revealed in *Jacks and Jokers*, former Director of Public Prosecutions, Des Sturgess, said he felt sorry for corrupt Commissioner Terry Lewis, and sprang to Williams's and Murphy's defence, saying that Williams did not need to involve himself in a fake raid as had been alleged. Sturgess defended the work of the Queensland police in the Werin Street raid, and said that in contrast the Narcotics Bureau's efforts in the matter had been ineffectual. Ultimately, Sturgess declared that Condon's accusation of Williams committing a criminal offence was ludicrous.

Many years later, Jim Slade told me, 'I have always been interested as to why we carried out this raid, with raiding police taking a large array and good quantity of drugs with them. The Werin Street raid! What a joke! No Narcs or Commonwealth police were present at that raid – this was the whole point, I believe Williams wanted to show how slack the Narcs were by not raiding. Queensland police raided the premises after receiving this letter from the commission.

'I am going to try and identify the occupants and show they were fitted up. I know they will say they did not own all the drugs they were arrested for. This had to be pre-planned by commission staff for Queensland Police to have taken such a keen interest in a single premises identified from a letter.'

Even a respected supreme court judge needed evidence

to support his recommendation to disband the Bureau, and the 'ineffectual efforts of the Narcotics Bureau over Werin Street' would provide such evidence. But bringing me into the Werin Street Incident in the royal commission hearing raised many questions. Had the raid been concocted to provide Williams with evidence to support his recommendation to disband the Bureau? Had Williams fabricated the letter, possibly in collusion with Murphy, but not told Hampson about his and Murphy's conspiracy? That may explain why it was Williams, not Hampson, who questioned me about this matter.

Prior to Milligan's arrest on 10 September, I'd never met him. After his arrest, the only time I was alone with him was when I was recording the Milligan Tapes on 12 and 13 September 1979. However, before his arrest, Milligan was frequently meeting and communicating with Hallahan, and Hallahan was in touch with his confidant Murphy. The Werin Street Incident was, according to Slade, Murphy's initiative. Surely Murphy would not have missed the opportunity to proudly boast to his mate Hallahan as to how he had 'set up' the Narcotics Bureau.

Despite this, in its *Report of the Australian Royal Commission of Inquiry into Drugs*, the Williams royal commission stated:

> It is difficult to understand how Milligan could have obtained information about this incident if Shobbrook or some other Narcotics agent did not tell him. Shobbrook's suggestion was that Milligan may have heard of the Werin Street incident from Glen Patrick Hallahan. The Commission does not accept this suggestion.

15

Sentenced

EARLY IN MARCH 1980, Milligan, having pleaded guilty to the Operation Jungle drug importation charges, appeared before Judge Barrie Thorley of the New South Wales District Court for sentencing. While I was presenting to the court the facts of the charge and Milligan's antecedents, Judge Thorley asked me, 'Why wasn't Hallahan arrested along with Milligan, Barron and Bridge?'

'The prosecution brief wasn't finished in relation to the man Hallahan,' I replied.

Judge Thorley returned his attention to Milligan, who stated from the dock that he was prepared to give evidence on behalf of the Crown against persons yet to be prosecuted for narcotics offences.

After Milligan made this comment, I quickly spoke to the Commonwealth Crown Solicitor, who in turn spoke to Michael Finnane, the barrister appearing for the Crown.

Finnane then asked Milligan, 'Who are you referring to when you say that you will give evidence for the Crown?'

'Bridge and Tak Tak,' Milligan answered. Tak Tak was the name of one of Milligan's Lebanese couriers.

'Are you prepared to give evidence against Glen Patrick Hallahan?' Finnane asked.

'Yes,' Milligan replied.

'Are you prepared to provide a statement to that effect?'

To this Milligan would not answer.

Judge Thorley paused, and then said, 'Well, Mr Milligan, I will postpone sentencing and remand you in custody for one week while you consider your answer to that question.'

The judge had just thrown me a much-needed life preserver. As Milligan was about to be returned to his cell at Long Bay, he told me that he would fully disclose Hallahan's involvement in a written and signed statement. This was the breakthrough I had been hoping for.

In view of Justice Williams's hostility towards me at his royal commission, it was decided that it would be best if I didn't obtain Milligan's written statement concerning Hallahan. On 18 March 1980, in response to the pressure applied by Judge Thorley of the Sydney District Court, Milligan wrote a five-page statement at Long Bay Gaol, which he handed to former Narcotics Agent Bill Harrigan, who like me was now an AFP officer. Milligan's statement, written on A4 blue notepaper, detailed Hallahan's involvement in the Jane Table Mountain heroin importation and claimed that:

- In 1977 Hallahan and Milligan discussed the importation of drugs by light aircraft into North Queensland.
- Hallahan agreed to finance a trip by one of Milligan's couriers, Bryan William Parker, to Thailand to purchase the heroin.
- In July 1977 Hallahan and Milligan met, at which time Hallahan gave Milligan $1,000, which in turn was to be given to Ian Robert Barron to charter a light aircraft to fly to New Guinea to acquaint Barron with flight details and Customs re-entry procedures back into Australia.
- Hallahan gave Milligan a further $500 towards the expense of Parker flying to New Guinea.
- When Barron reported to Milligan that a drug importation by light aircraft from New Guinea to Australia would be possible, Milligan telephoned this information to Hallahan.
- Milligan met with Hallahan at a service station at Nambour, Queensland, where Milligan was handed a further $3,000 by Hallahan, which was to be used by Parker to purchase the heroin in Thailand.
- On 15 September 1977, Milligan telephoned Hallahan at Obi Obi to report that Parker had arrived in New Guinea with the heroin.
- Hallahan was again telephoned when the heroin was dropped onto the mountain north of Cairns.
- Milligan met Hallahan at Mapleton (near Obi Obi), north of Brisbane, and informed Hallahan of the difficulty that was being encountered in recovering

the heroin. Hallahan ordered Milligan to keep looking for it.

- Milligan eventually found one of the two heroin parcels that had been dropped from the light aircraft. This was taken to Sydney and sold.
- Some of the money, $26,000, from the sale of that heroin was transferred to the bank account of G.P. Hallahan, Commonwealth Trading Bank, King George Square, Brisbane.

Milligan's handwritten statement became Confidential Exhibit 471 at the Williams royal commission.

On 19 March 1980, Milligan was sentenced at Sydney's District Court of Criminal Jurisdiction by Judge Thorley to eighteen years' imprisonment with hard labour on three charges related to heroin importation. He was given a non-parole period of nine years, with the sentence to date from the time of his arrest in September 1979.

The charges that Milligan pleaded guilty to and was convicted of were: conspiracy to import a quantity of heroin into Australia between January and May 1977 (the heroin importation by Richard Mallouhi using a false-bottomed suitcase); knowingly concerned in the importation of a prohibited import in 1979 (an importation of heroin from New Caledonia); and conspiracy to import a quantity of heroin into Australia between January and October 1977 (the Jane Table Mountain heroin importation).

In the case of Jane Table, I had charged Milligan with conspiracy to import, as opposed to the actual importation of the heroin, because the 'conspiracy' to import the heroin had been agreed upon between Milligan, Hallahan, Barron, Bridge and Parker in New South Wales, whereas the actual importation had occurred in Queensland. I wanted Milligan, and especially Hallahan, to appear before a New South Wales court, where Hallahan and his police friends could bring less corrupt influence to bear. The conspiracy charge moved the jurisdiction from Queensland to New South Wales. Ian Robert Barron and Graham David Bridge were each subsequently sentenced to five years' imprisonment.

Sometime after Milligan's sentencing, an officer from the Commonwealth Crown Solicitor's Office in Sydney discreetly informed me that Judge Thorley had said that, when Hallahan finally came to trial, he wanted the matter listed before him. All I needed to do was complete the brief of evidence against Hallahan. I had already been told by the Crown Solicitor's Office in Brisbane that I had sufficient evidence to place him before a magistrate for a committal hearing that would decide if he should face trial for heroin importation.

I began to believe that there was a light at the end of the tunnel. Little did I know that it was the headlight of a train coming the other way, and that Royal Commissioner Williams himself was driving it.

16

The Findings

ON 20 MARCH 1980, Milligan made his third and final appearance in the witness box at the Williams royal commission. On this occasion he was questioned by Hampson about an undercover operation against him conducted by the New South Wales Police Drug Squad in July 1979.

I had written about this matter to the royal commission at their request, and provided a summary of all items the Narcotics Bureau held that gave rise to the belief that Hallahan and Milligan were jointly involved in illegal activities relating to narcotics trafficking. My eight-page typewritten document, containing thirty-seven paragraphs of allegations against Hallahan, was dated 10 March 1980.

One of the allegations was as follows. In July 1979, soon after his release from Long Bay Gaol, Milligan began planning a heroin importation from Manila in the Philippines. The New South Wales Drug Squad had managed to insert an undercover police officer, a woman using the alias Sue White, into Milligan's orbit, and he intended to use her as his drug courier for this job.

Milligan, White and an informant named McGovern met at a hotel in Pitt Street, Sydney, to discuss the importation, and Milligan decided to call a contact to verify that White would not be stopped when she re-entered Australia with the heroin. 'It is believed that MILLIGAN was to use HALLAHAN on this occasion to check the name being used by the courier,' I had written in my summary for the commission, 'to ensure that she wasn't recorded on any Police or Customs watch lists at the airport.'

McGovern watched Milligan dial the number, then left the room on the pretext that he needed cigarettes. Outside, he wrote down the phone number 469 126. As I stated for the commission, '469 125 is the telephone number of HALLAHAN at Obi Obi'. McGovern had made an error with the final digit but it was clear whom Milligan was contacting.

Six months later, at the royal commission, Hampson was interrogating Milligan about this. 'The point about trying to contact Canberra, this man,' Hampson said, 'was to discover whether, if she went out as a courier and got drugs and came back via Manila, there would be an alert on her in the Customs computer.'

Sitting in the courtroom, I recoiled in shock. Milligan had not attempted to contact 'some man in Canberra' – he had called former detective sergeant Hallahan at his home in

Obi Obi, Queensland. My report to the royal commission had made this clear.

Hampson had obviously read my report, as he got all the other details correct: that the name to be checked was that of a woman, that she was to be used as a courier, that she would be bringing back drugs, not some other form of illegal import, and that she would be returning from Manila. The only detail Hampson had altered was to insert some anonymous person in Canberra in place of Hallahan.

From that day forward, the official transcript of the Williams royal commission, at page 25505, would record that 'Canberra, this man' was standing by to assist Milligan during a heroin importation, rather than the subscriber to telephone number 469 125.

This was not a slip-up by one of the greatest legal minds in Queensland. This was deliberate. It was Milligan's third visit to the royal commission's witness box, and Hampson knew he wouldn't correct him and name Hallahan in open court. Hampson had tampered with my evidence with the clear objective of protecting Hallahan.

As Milligan's evidence was concluding, Hampson directly asked him if he had any information involving Hallahan in relation to drug trafficking. As expected, in the open court, Milligan replied, 'No.'

Sitting on the bar table in front of Hampson was an A4 pad of blue paper with handwriting on it: the statement Milligan had penned naming Hallahan as his co-conspirator. I assumed Hampson would proceed to confront Milligan with his own words about Hallahan, but instead Hampson paused for a moment, appearing to gather his thoughts, then said, 'No further questions, Your Honour.'

I wanted to get up and shout, 'What about the bloody blue notepad?' Milligan's handwritten statement, Confidential Exhibit 471, sat forlornly on the bar table. Those two giants of the Queensland legal system, Williams and Hampson, had stopped Milligan from publicly referring to his detailed signed statement that incriminated Hallahan. Not one of Milligan's allegations against Hallahan saw the light of day at the Australian Royal Commission of Inquiry into Drugs.

I felt shell-shocked. Their intent to discredit me and Operation Jungle was clear, but I couldn't understand why Williams and Hampson would want to stick their necks out to save Hallahan when everybody knew that he was a crook.

Years later, when I met with former detective Jim Slade, who was a key source for the ground-breaking 'Moonlight State' program that helped spark the 1987–89 Fitzgerald inquiry (more formally titled the Commission of Inquiry into Possible Illegal Activities and Associated Police Misconduct), I asked him, 'Why did Williams want to protect Glen Hallahan?'

Slade's reply was brief: 'They weren't protecting Hallahan, John, they were protecting Terry Lewis.'

Given that Lewis was the Commissioner of the Queensland Police Force at that time, what Slade was telling me was that the Williams royal commission was protecting the Queensland police.

But there were several immediate reasons as to why the commissioner and his counsel assisting acted so boldly as to exonerate Hallahan in the face of considerable evidence condemning him.

In spite of the disbanding of the Narcotics Bureau, I was still a law-enforcement officer and now very close to arresting Hallahan. Williams and Hampson were acutely aware of this and needed to act without delay. This is why they attacked my credibility as an investigator from the first day of the hearings and trivialised Milligan's role as a reliable source of information.

By negating my reliability as a law-enforcement officer in the eyes of the AFP, Williams and Hampson, both members of the Queensland 'old boys club', not only neutralised me, but were also in a position to do a big favour for the Queensland Police Force, and for the Queensland premier.

Queensland Premier Joh Bjelke-Petersen was no lover of anything 'federal'. He would be furious with any adverse publicity generated should the Federal Police arrest a long-time associate of the police commissioner for importing heroin. A police commissioner that he had personally chosen. If they could prevent this, then he would be in Williams's and Hampson's debt.

Williams and Hampson also knew that Hallahan, if arrested and interrogated, might be the first domino to fall. If Hallahan fell, how many others might he sacrifice in a deal to protect his own skin? Hallahan was close to falling, but unfortunately, with a push from the AFP, so was I.

There is every possibility that Williams did believe

I was corrupt – I wasn't, but he could have been led to that impression by the investigators assisting him. When the Williams royal commission was established, it had set up its own small team of investigators who assisted the commissioner by interviewing witnesses and gathering evidence. It initially chose Commonwealth police and later Queensland police officers as members of this team. No Narcotics agents were included, which was odd for a royal commission into drugs. (Only later, after the Bureau had been disbanded and when the commission began investigating allegations of politicians' involvement in the drug trade in Queensland, did it bring two former Narcotics Bureau officers, Ray Phillips and Bill Harrigan, onto its investigative team.)

Given that there were three Queensland Police Force detectives on the royal commission's team, it's plausible that they were massaging the evidence coming into the commission, and possibly advising Williams and Hampson that I was on some corrupt crusade against honest Queensland police. But Williams and Hampson would have to have been living in a vacuum to not know of Hallahan's reputation or of the Rat Pack.

One of the men approved by Williams to assist his commission, apparently on the recommendation of Police Commissioner Terry Lewis, was Detective Sergeant Barrie O'Brien from the Queensland Police Force. (O'Brien would later be named adversely at the Fitzgerald inquiry.) I had known O'Brien for some time before the commission, and, as I was returning to my office one afternoon after giving evidence, I ran into him in the street.

'You are ratshit with the Queensland Police Force!' he informed me venomously.

I didn't lose any sleep over his opinion. I knew I had done nothing improper during my investigations, or during the interviews I had conducted with Milligan, but I was fearful of the power of Williams and Hampson, and the whole matter caused me and my wife, Jan, a great deal of stress. Yet I remained confident in the evidence that Caswell, Moller and I had discovered, and I remained confident that justice would prevail.

Despite the lack of support I was receiving from my own organisation, I pressed on with my investigations into the activities of Milligan and Hallahan. On 26 March 1980, in a report sent to the Officer in Charge, Narcotics Operations, Northern Division, I wrote:

Attached is a report completed on 10th March, 1980, which deals with those items giving rise to the belief that Glen Patrick Hallahan and John Edward Milligan are jointly involved in illegal narcotics activities.

I believe that the investigation should be continued in relation to HALLAHAN'S involved [sic] in this importation and that the investigation should concentrate on the Jane Table aspect, which presents the greatest volume of circumstantial evidence at this stage.

The attached report has been read by Mr Thomas Q.C., counsel representing the Department of Administrative Services before the Federal Royal Commission, and Mr G. Spender, barrister, counsel representing the A.P.S.A.

[Australian Public Service Association] before the Federal Royal Commission. Both have commented that, having read the report, they feel that the department already has a basis of a sound prosecution case against Glen Hallahan. The question of Hallahan has also been discussed with Mr M. Finnane, barrister, counsel briefed by the Crown in the prosecutions of Milligan, Bridge and Barron. Mr Finnane again has stated the continued investigation into Hallahan should receive immediate attention.

I also requested that a member of the ACT police's Fraud Squad assist me with my investigation of Hallahan's financial situation.

When my request reached Central Office in Canberra, they contacted Regional Commander Ray Cooper and ordered him to terminate the Operation Jungle investigation. Cooper told me that the explanation given was that I was 'too personally involved'. It was of interest that no other officer, someone less 'personally involved', was asked to continue the investigation.

The following month, on 17 April 1980, Royal Commissioner Williams released his findings regarding the evidence I had presented of Hallahan's involvement in the illicit drugs trade in his report to the Queensland Government:

The Commission merely records that evidence presently available to it falls far short of establishing as even a reasonable possibility, that Hallahan has ever been involved in wrong-doing in connection with illegal drugs.

Williams and Hampson had not only cleared Hallahan's name, but they had also done their best to brand me as a bumbling, incompetent and naive investigator obsessed with arresting the Queensland commissioner of police. Further, they had suggested I was prepared to falsify evidence in an attempt to bring down honest Queensland police officers.

The day after Williams's findings were announced, the Brisbane *Telegraph* printed a photograph of a beaming Hallahan confirming that he had never been involved in wrongdoing in connection with illegal drugs. 'The suggestion that I am still under investigation is wrong,' he stated. 'If there was any evidence connecting me with any wrongdoing of any sort, somebody would have done something about it by now!'

Believe me, Glen, I tried.

17

The End

By the time Commissioner Williams released his findings, my career in the AFP was not going smoothly. I was the second-highest-ranking federal narcotics investigator in Queensland and the Northern Territory, yet no ongoing investigations were assigned to me. I had stubbornly refused to read the writing on the wall, despite the fact that it was now spelling out the path my career would take.

Noel Caswell remained in the AFP until 1996 and went on to attain the rank of detective superintendent. John Moller did not receive an employment offer to continue as a police officer in the AFP but was attached to their Intelligence Section – I suspect this was payback for his talkback radio initiative. Moller ended his law-enforcement career and eventually took up a position at The University of Queensland.

Technically, my new boss was now former Commonwealth police superintendent Bob Gillespie. During previous visits to his office, I was amazed at the number of diplomas that lined his office walls. Perhaps this indicated the path to advancement in the new force? I suspected that the former Commonwealth Police Force, whose members now comprised the bulk of the AFP, put a higher priority (rightly or wrongly) on tertiary qualifications as opposed to investigative skills. I'd left school at fourteen, and I didn't have a high school certificate, let alone any tertiary qualifications. And so, in February 1980, I enrolled as a part-time 'mature-age' student in a Bachelor of Arts degree at The University of Queensland. My goal was to achieve sufficient grades in Arts so that I could qualify for admission to a combined Arts/Law degree.

The threats my senior colleague had made that I would be 'buried' were being realised. I hadn't been physically moved to a stores branch, but neither had I been given investigation or supervision duties. I sat behind an empty desk with the familiar sounds of the office going on around me, but I was no longer a part of that office. I had nothing to do and all the time in the world to do it. The rest of the staff virtually ignored me, and I don't blame them. They had also gone through Williams's torment – some no longer had a role in active law enforcement and would now be clerical officers in the public service. I tried to look for the silver lining in the cloud that hung over me and decided to spend my time in the office on my university studies. While my fellow officers went about their investigations, I filled my empty desk with textbooks on anthropology, geography, ancient history and astronomy.

Just when I thought I had found a way to be taken seriously in my position by obtaining a university degree, and felt I could work towards a future in the AFP, a trivial incident ended it all. On 3 April 1980, a document dealing with a clerical matter arrived from Central Office via our telex machine. The document directed me to ask all staff for suggestions on how to improve the security arrangements in our office.

I was the type of officer who had always taken these requests seriously. In the past, I would have thought through the directive and offered suggestions. But now the reality of my situation following the royal commission and disbanding of the Narcotics Bureau flashed before me in blinding neon: *What's the point? Who'd act on any suggestions that came from Shobbrook? Face it — it's over.*

I realised that I'd lost respect for the organisation that I worked for, and that this organisation had little respect for me. I doubted the integrity of my senior officers, who had effectively shredded two years of investigation. A royal commission had branded me a liar and a fool. Other law-enforcement agencies wanted nothing to do with me. For me, the dust would never settle. There would be no bright future in law enforcement in Queensland for John Shobbrook.

I dropped the telex onto my desk, put my head in my hands and surrendered. 'They've won,' I repeatedly sobbed. 'They've won.'

Senior Narcotics Agent Doug Cogill and Narcotics Agent Alan Jones heard my sobs and came into my office. One of them put his hand on my shoulder and said, 'We'll call Jan.' When she arrived in a state of confusion and concern, Ray Cooper gently said, 'I think you'd better take him home.'

After a few weeks at home on sick leave, during which time I was depressed and worried with no idea where my future lay, on 24 June 1980, I was officially sworn in to the AFP. They then moved swiftly to correct their mistake, and made an appointment for me to be assessed by the Australian Government's consulting psychiatrist, Dr David Webster. Following my consultation, the Commonwealth Employees' Compensation Branch asked Dr Webster, 'Did Mr Shobbrook's condition pre-date his employment with the Australian Federal Police?'

In his reply, Dr Webster wrote:

> The answer to this question is that Mr Shobbrook was entirely asymptomatic when he joined the Federal Police (Narcotics Bureau). He had the sort of personality type which made him vulnerable. I believe that the very factors which made Mr Shobbrook vulnerable also made him a very efficient officer with the Federal Police. I believe that Mr Shobbrook brought to his position in the Federal Police a great deal of enthusiasm, dedication and idealism. When he was faced with a situation which he could not reconcile with his expectations, then he decompensated. I would not comment as to whether the obstacles which Mr Shobbrook met with were real.

I believe that the very characteristics which made him such an efficient officer, and which led to his promotion in the Federal Police, made him a very attractive recruit to the Force. There is no doubt that the happenings within the Federal Police and Shobbrook's experiences there, led to his decompensation. There appear to be no factors outside his employment that I have been able to discover which led to his decompensation. I would not wish to enter into the debate as to whether Mr Shobbrook was right in his assessment of certain criminal activities or not. He certainly presents strong evidence to support his belief.

Dr Webster played it straight down the line and offered no personal opinions. However, as I was about to leave his office following my consultation, he handed me a yellow Post-it note upon which he had written: 'Read Matthew 5: Blessed are you when you are persecuted.'

A few days later, I received a telephone call at home from Carol Cooper, a former colleague at the Narcotics Bureau who was now working in the AFP's Personnel Section. No doubt as surprised as I was, Cooper discreetly informed me that the Commonwealth Medical Officer had recommended that I be permanently superannuated out of the Commonwealth Public Service as being 'medically unfit'.

And so, without setting foot inside the new AFP headquarters, and at only thirty-two years of age, I had progressed within one month from being sworn in to the AFP to being found to be 'medically unfit to discharge the duties of a member of the Australian Federal Police'.

Further, on 22 July 1980, I received a letter from the AFP's Acting Assistant Commissioner, W.L. Antill, which read:

As a consequence of you undergoing medical examinations, I have been advised that you are unfit to discharge the duties of your position as a member of the Police Force or any other position in the Police Force.

As delegate of the Minister, it is my responsibility under Section 38(2) of the *Australian Federal Police Act 1979* to determine whether you should be retired from the Police Force. Before doing so, I have decided you should be given the opportunity to put forward in writing any matters which you wish me to consider in taking my decision.

I would appreciate your response in this matter within seven days of the date of this letter.

W.L. Antill

In my reply of 29 July 1980, I said:

I refer to your letter of the 22nd of July, 1980 and wish to comment as follows.

On the 20th of February, 1980 I was discreetly informed by a senior member of the Australian Federal Police that I should consider leaving the Australian Federal Police Force as the Force did not require 'crusading investigators'. I was told that should I choose to remain in the Force, I would be denied promotion and restricted in my future duties.

I chose to remain in the Force believing that Force to stand for high principles and knowing that I had committed no offence apart from conducting my investigations without fear or favour.

A couple of weeks after making the decision to stay with the Australian Federal Police, the threats of that senior officer were put into effect. I was denied promotion to an acting position which I had satisfactorily filled on two previous occasions and I was instructed to cease my investigations on a major drug trafficking syndicate which I had been investigating continuously for the previous thirteen months with considerable success.

I now find myself unable to come down to the standards of the Australian Federal Police and am surprised that, prior to this general letter, no senior member of the Australian Federal Police has wished to discuss this situation with me.

I wish the new Force well in its endeavours to combat the growing Australian drug problem.

Yours faithfully,

D.J. Shobbrook

These were serious allegations that I was placing before Assistant Commissioner Antill. I received neither a written nor a verbal reply, from him or from anyone else.

After almost eleven years of intensive training, experience and dedicated service to Australia's illegal drugs law-enforcement effort, I was superannuated out of the AFP and informed that I was suffering from an 'acute situational crisis'. At no time did the AFP consider whether – if I was genuinely 'medically unfit' – a period of convalescence might restore my health and eventually return me to duty. My career as a law-enforcement officer was officially terminated on 29 October 1980.

Having been discharged from the AFP, and with no further access to the evidence that I had gathered over the previous two years, and no knowledge of whether that evidence had suffered the fate that had been recommended for Greg Rainbow's original heroin seizure from Dave Ward – destruction in a furnace – I was now powerless to take any action against Hallahan or any other police officer who was criminally involved in Operation Jungle.

But I could still talk to people in power or people with influence – people who I trusted – and warn them about the corruption that I knew existed within the highest ranks of the Queensland Police Force and the Queensland judiciary. I could alert them to the AFP's unwillingness to take action against that corruption, which was also a sign of corruption within the AFP. If I did so, I risked prosecution under the *Official Secrets Act*, but I suspected that nobody in government would be willing to make a public issue of this.

Around 1982, I telephoned the office of Senator Don Chipp, the leader of the Australian Democrats, then the third-largest political party in Australia. Chipp was a former Minister for Customs and Excise in Liberal governments, and had been instrumental in establishing the Federal Bureau of Narcotics. I believe I initially spoke to Chipp's Democrats colleague Senator John Siddons. I advised him that I was a former member of the Narcotics Bureau, and that a former Queensland police officer's involvement in a major heroin importation was being covered up by the AFP and the Williams royal commission. A short time later I received a call back from Senator Chipp's office, and was advised of arrangements that had been made so that I could meet with Senator Chipp in Brisbane.

Don Chipp appeared to enjoy the cloak-and-dagger aspect of our meeting. He booked into a motel in the Brisbane northside suburb of Boondall using the name 'Mr Leslie' (his middle name). I thought that this was odd as Senator Chipp had one of the most recognisable faces in Australia, and I felt slightly embarrassed when I asked at reception which room Mr Leslie was in. I believe the receptionist was stifling a grin as she directed me to his room.

I gave Chipp a detailed briefing on Operation Jungle, and on the Williams royal commission's exoneration of Hallahan. I also supplied him with a suitcase full of documentation to support my claims. As I did so, the thought crossed my mind that I could go to jail for the action I was taking.

Chipp was extremely interested. He listened quietly, and from time to time nodded his head or asked a clarifying question. He did not challenge my belief that this investigation had been prematurely terminated. In fact, he told me that it wasn't the first time that he had heard some of the information that I was outlining to him. After a couple of hours our meeting concluded, then he thanked me and I left the motel. I never met 'Mr Leslie' again.

Following our meeting, Senator Chipp forwarded a copy of my Operation Jungle allegations to Justice Donald Stewart, who was conducting a Royal Commission of Inquiry into Drug Trafficking on behalf of the Commonwealth and the three eastern mainland states. Justice Stewart criticised the fact that this information had been forwarded to him, and told Chipp, 'Don't give me evidence submitted by amateurs.' His advice to Senator Chipp was that he 'should make that information available to the Queensland Police or the Australian Federal Police'.

Here we go again, I thought. *Pass the information to the two organisations that needed investigating!* But then I discovered that one of the Stewart royal commission's team of nine investigators was none other than Barrie O'Brien. No doubt O'Brien would take every opportunity to argue to Stewart that Williams and Hampson had found my evidence untrustworthy and considered it to have been fabricated.

Despite the pushback from the Stewart royal commission, in a speech to the Senate on 25 March 1982 concerning a Joint Task Force on Drug Trafficking report dealing with matters arising from the activities of the drug-trafficking Nugan Hand Bank, Senator Chipp said:

> I do not relish the thought of being the sole defender in this nation of the former Narcotics Bureau. But I am its defender and proud to be. Of course there were crooked officers in the Narcotics Bureau, particularly in the latter years. The disbandment of the Federal Bureau of Narcotics was announced in this Parliament [...] at

precisely the time the Melbourne Cup was run. I do not regard that as fortuitous. Something stinks about the reason why the Federal Bureau of Narcotics was disbanded. The thing that stinks is the stench that comes from the Queensland Police Force [...] [which] would be one of the most corrupt, rotten and contemptible groups of people engaged in law enforcement in the world at this time.

There is something that stinks and I hope that this task force can get to it. I hope that its report will be better than the comparatively useless report of the Williams Commission and the Woodward Commission. If ever there was a joke, a total waste of public money, a waste of at least hundreds of thousands of dollars – I think it got to millions of dollars – it was the compilation of the Woodward and Williams reports. The dogs in Sydney and Brisbane are barking, yet a judge, sitting as a commissioner, cannot find it.

It is a sad day when those persons who are courageous enough to bring the evidence to the one branch of officialdom where it might do some good – the royal commission – are made to feel that they have acted foolishly or precipitately.

Years later I lost most of my possessions in a bushfire, but one of the few items from that time that I still have is a copy of Don Chipp's autobiography. He inscribed it for me thus: 'To John Shobbrook. A remarkable man of the highest integrity and incorruptible courage with best wishes from an admirer. Don Chipp.'

On 29 November 1985, I received a letter from the Commonwealth Employees' Compensation Branch requesting details of my 'illness' from my 'treating doctor'. I was angered by the Commonwealth's obvious continuing cover-up of the facts surrounding my departure from the AFP. In replying to the Officer-in-Charge of the Compensation Branch, I summarised my case:

> How many senior Federal officers have turned a blind eye to the truth of this matter? [...] Do you have the courage to personally initiate action against those still serving senior Australian Federal Police officers, and others, who through acts of commission or omission, forced me out of my career and at the same time allowed a major narcotics trafficker (and heaven knows how many associates) to avoid prosecution?

Rather than putting anything in writing, the Compensation Branch telephoned me and advised that I would no longer be required to submit myself for regular medical examinations. I was correct in my previous belief: the government didn't want to make a public issue of this.

Despite the attempted cover-ups of the events that led to me being discharged from the AFP, over the years that followed the truth began to surface. During December 1986 and January 1987, *The Courier-Mail* published a series of articles, written by Phil Dickie, about vice and police inactivity in Queensland. Similar allegations had been made previously without provoking any reaction.

However, on 11 May 1987, ABC TV's *Four Corners* program broadcast a report by Chris Masters titled 'The Moonlight State'. This program included clandestinely recorded footage, which raised the real possibility that the Queensland Police Force was lying or incompetent – or both.

The day after 'The Moonlight State' was broadcast, Queensland's acting premier, Bill Gunn, announced that there would be an inquiry. The general belief was that this new inquiry would go nowhere, and that it was primarily a means of easing the political pressure on the government. However, the appointment of a courageous commissioner ensured that wouldn't be the case.

Following the announcement of the inquiry, and before Commissioner Tony Fitzgerald QC commenced taking evidence, both Phil Dickie and Chris Masters contacted me in the hope that I would speak to them. I was happy to speak to them, so I met Dickie at his flat in New Farm, and then Masters at the Tower Mill Hotel in the city.

On 24 September 1987, I contacted the offices of the Fitzgerald inquiry and subsequently supplied them with a forty-two-page statement addressing the evidence of police corruption that I had gathered some eight years previously. They agreed that I had provided sufficient evidence to support charges being brought against Hallahan – charges that they said should have been laid by the AFP in 1980.

I gave evidence to the inquiry in camera at their office at 95 North Quay, Brisbane. I repeated the testimony that I had sworn before Justice Williams, Hampson and their royal commission, with the addition of what had happened to my career at the hands of the AFP following the release of Williams's findings.

I hadn't requested that my evidence be taken in private, and I wondered why I hadn't been asked to give it in open court. Then I learnt that the counsel appearing for the Queensland Police Force at the Fitzgerald inquiry was none other than Cedric Hampson QC. Seven years after he'd exonerated Hallahan and ended my career, you can imagine the sparks that would have flown between him and me – and the claims I would have made about him from the witness box – had we come face to face. I would have welcomed the opportunity, with the media present, to remind Hampson of his past crimes.

But the Fitzgerald inquiry hadn't kept us apart to protect Hampson; they were working to a deadline, and were busy with the recent rollover by Jack Herbert, who had confessed to being a bagman for the corrupt Commissioner of Police, Terry Lewis. Understandably, Fitzgerald didn't want the flow of his inquiry to be interrupted by an almighty confrontation between one of his witnesses and the counsel defending the Queensland Police Force.

Finally, on 9 August 1988, Phil Dickie wrote an article in *The Courier-Mail* newspaper headlined 'Milligan's Mountain'. It stated that Fitzgerald inquiry investigators were examining the links between Milligan and Hallahan, and supplied details of the Operation Jungle investigation, and in particular details of the interaction between Milligan and Hallahan. The article claimed that a spokesperson for the AFP had specifically denied that the Operation Jungle investigation had been terminated on 26 March 1980 because it may have affected cooperation with the Queensland police. The AFP spokesperson said, 'It had nothing to do with Queensland Police cooperation. There was insufficient evidence at the time for the investigation to proceed, it wasn't just the AFP's opinion, we received the same advice from the Director of Public Prosecutions.' Much to the spokesperson's embarrassment and confusion, Phil Dickie pointed out that they were talking about events in 1980, and that the office of Director of Public Prosecutions was not established until March 1984.

At the conclusion of my evidence to the Fitzgerald inquiry, Robert Marxson, a legal officer assisting the inquiry, telephoned me at home. He thanked me for giving evidence to the inquiry and added, 'We believe you this time, Mr Shobbrook.'

Afterword

by Quentin Dempster

So, THAT IS HOW John Shobbrook was destroyed. That is how the Federal Bureau of Narcotics, an agency established in 1969 by John Gorton's Coalition government to confront Australia's burgeoning market in imported illicit drugs, then mainly heroin, was subverted.

With a stubborn refusal by most Australian governments to decriminalise recreational drug use, the illicit drug trade remains a significant criminal activity today. Our failures in preventative health and drugs policy over the decades have been well documented, but the criminal compromise of law enforcement exposed in this book is just as disturbing. We need honest cops to protect the community, particularly from the criminality of their own colleagues.

Operation Jungle provided early evidence of police corruption in drug trafficking. The investigation identified Glen Hallahan, a former Queensland detective, as the organiser of a significant drug importation. Shobbrook also had the self-incriminating testimony of drug trafficker John Edward Milligan, who appeared to have enjoyed police protection in both New South Wales and Queensland until the Narcotics Bureau's agents knocked on his door.

Through Milligan, the evidence against Hallahan was extensive, probative and admissible in court. It included hire-car and aircraft-rental records, accommodation receipts, telephone records, statements from eye-witnesses, and payments from and to Hallahan at the times and places Milligan had detailed.

That brief of evidence – compiled after a 'shoe leather' investigation and complemented by Milligan's confessional tape-recorded interviews, and his five-page handwritten statement – was compelling. Shobbrook had the advice of the Commonwealth Crown Solicitor that Hallahan's arrest and prosecution for the Jane Table importation alone was justified, and there was more in Milligan's testimony that would require investigation, including Milligan's and Hallahan's other drug importations, and the broader allegation that Hallahan enjoyed protection through his membership of what Milligan called 'the Triumvirate': Hallahan, Police Commissioner Terry Lewis and Assistant Commissioner Tony Murphy.

Although Milligan was hesitant to name individuals on tape, he described to Shobbrook how certain people had assisted him in his criminal activities through their positions in police forces or government departments, including an officer in the passport office who had helped him obtain false passports. Shobbrook was stunned when

Milligan named Shobbrook's former Narcotics Bureau boss Max Rogers as having tipped him off that an investigation into his activities, codenamed 'Operation Jungle', was underway.

Hallahan should have been arrested and charged, with the law and consequent investigations allowed to take their course. In any competent and professional law-enforcement agency, a special task force would have pursued all the leads to corruption and criminality. Who knows how the investigation would have concluded if Shobbrook's evidence had come to a competent and professional agency? Perhaps, under the plea bargain processes, Hallahan himself may have been persuaded to tell all he knew about police corruption.

Instead, the weight of the world came down on the Narcotics Bureau. Shobbrook found himself aggressively interrogated by the Williams royal commission into drugs, and abandoned by his superiors before and after the Bureau was wound up, and its staff absorbed into the newly formed Australian Federal Police (AFP).

How could this have happened? How could Milligan's inconvenient naming of the Rat Pack police officers – Terry Lewis, Tony Murphy and Glen Hallahan – be covered up by a duly constituted royal commission with investigative resources?

The answer lies in history. The three Rat Packers were among eighty-eight police officers represented by legal counsel at the National Hotel royal commission, established in 1963 to investigate allegations that leading police officers, including Police Commissioner Frank Bischof, 'frequent the National Hotel, encouraging and condoning the call-girl service that operates there'. Then Queensland Supreme Court judge Harry Talbot Gibbs made a blind-eyed finding that 'no member of the Police Force [...] has been guilty of misconduct or neglect or violation of duty' in policing activities at the National Hotel, that 'no call-girl service was operated at the said hotel', and that 'no member of the police force encouraged, condoned or sanctioned in any way the practice of prostitution at that hotel'.

In the decade that followed, corrupt police in Queensland and elsewhere were not contrite about having escaped exposure by a royal commission – they were emboldened. And for thirteen years, until Shobbrook arrested Milligan and was about to arrest Hallahan, they were in covert comfort. Eventually they were exposed through the Fitzgerald Commission of Inquiry into Possible Illegal Activities and Associated Police Misconduct.

To overcome the forensic disadvantage caused by the police culture's well-known 'code of silence', Commissioner Tony Fitzgerald QC and his investigators used innovative tactics. Indemnified from prosecution, Jack Herbert, the 'bagman' for police bribes, rolled over and named Lewis, Murphy, Hallahan and dozens of other serving and former police officers. Herbert called police corruption 'The Joke', and described a system in which bribe money was collected from SP bookmakers, prostitute services and a gaming machine operator and distributed to police who were in on the deal, up to and including the commissioner of police.

A special prosecutor was set up to criminally charge many serving and former Queensland police officers, assisted by the evidence produced by Herbert's confession and the confessions of other indemnified police. Terry Lewis was convicted on fifteen counts of corruption when his meticulous, incriminating diaries were finally admitted into evidence after legal argument. He was sentenced to fourteen years' imprisonment, and stripped of his knighthood and other honours.

Tony Murphy, having escaped a National Hotel perjury prosecution after the death of prostitute Shirley Brifman in 1972, was never charged with any criminal offence. He died in December 2010. Under British justice, he continues to enjoy, as they say, the presumption of innocence.

By 1989, Fitzgerald had at last cracked the police code of silence in Australia, which was no mean feat given the cynicism, expediency and manipulative cunning of the corrupt police culture. The inquiry also cracked the cosy relationship between police and journalists, many of whom thought that drinking in pubs with cops all day was real journalism. Police reporters were exposed as easily led, with some publishing sensational but lethal misinformation from their corrupt police 'sources'.

In New South Wales, the Royal Commission into the New South Wales Police Service built on the Fitzgerald inquiry's coercive and investigative tactics between 1995 and 1997. Counsel Assisting Justice James Roland Wood QC was Gary Crooke QC, who had assisted Fitzgerald in Queensland. Bent coppers laughed as the Wood royal commission offered an amnesty if they came forward to confess their corruption, but one indemnified police officer, Trevor Haken, was wired for sound and video as he distributed bribe money to his police associates, and the endemic corruption of the New South Wales Police Force was thus exposed.

It is regrettable that the Fitzgerald inquiry did not expose the second cover-up in Queensland – the one facilitated by the Williams royal commission. Fitzgerald has indicated that he could have gone on for years, but after the Jack Herbert revelations had exposed the enormity of the problem, he was anxious to wind up while he still had the political support of Mike Ahern's National Party government, which was willing to set up a new accountability system for Queensland. Although Counsel Assisting Robert Marxson took lengthy details from Shobbrook concerning Commissioner Williams's failure to follow the Milligan leads, the Fitzgerald inquiry chose not to open that Pandora's box.

The Williams cover-up started through what appears, on the surface, to be the manipulation of insular jurisdictional rivalries. The Federal Bureau of Narcotics was straying into Queensland and New South Wales police areas of operations in drug law enforcement, claiming a Commonwealth responsibility at the Customs barrier. Still in its infancy, the Bureau was finding its way in catching and prosecuting illicit drug importers. It was headed by Harvey Bates, a dedicated Customs man who had gained a favourable reputation by rooting out corruption within Customs employees on the wharves of Melbourne and Sydney. Bates had always wanted Customs to have a stronger law-enforcement capacity.

By the 1970s, the domestic drugs market was of great

public concern, with the media speculating about the existence of a 'Mr Big'. In 1977 the New South Wales government established the Woodward Royal Commission into Drug Trafficking, following the disappearance of anti-drugs campaigner Donald Mackay. Milligan was named through that commission's examination of known Australian drug traffickers who had been through the criminal courts or were already persons of interest to police. Milligan's trips to Thailand and Port Moresby to facilitate the postage of heroin were noted by Woodward, but not pursued.

Shobbrook has described in vivid detail how he came to lead Operation Jungle, the Bureau's investigation, formally initiated on 4 January 1979, into the Jane Table Mountain importation of September to October 1977. Coincidentally and tragically parallel, it now can be said, was the Williams Royal Commission of Inquiry into Drugs, which was established on 13 October 1977 and would run for several years. The terms of reference required the commission to enquire into and report on the extent of, and methods and places used, in the illegal production, importation, export and trafficking in drugs. The commission was to identify 'persons who engage, on an organised basis, in other illegal activities, whether or not related to drugs'.

Undertaking this task were two of Queensland's finest: Justice Edward (Ned) Stratten Williams QC, and leading barrister Cedric Edward Keid Hampson QC. Both had served their country in war and both were highly regarded and dripping with professional and community honours. Williams was a horse racing man and supreme court judge, while Hampson, a leader of the Queensland Bar with a gruff persona and determined advocacy, had a formidable reputation for his courtroom cross-examinations for the defence.

They set to their task with a will, talking to police commissioners, premiers, ministers and relevant public officials, and embarking on a world tour, visiting the United States, Canada, Chile, Argentina, Brazil, Peru, Mexico, Hong Kong, Singapore, Thailand, 'Burma', Indonesia and Malaysia. While in London, Williams had inspected drug-detection facilities at Heathrow Airport, and had many informal discussions with known drug-detection and rehabilitation experts.

The first indication that the Williams and Hampson sleuths had been diverted in their efforts to identify 'persons who engage in organised illicit drug activities' was when they declined to appoint to their investigations staff any officer from the Narcotics Bureau. Something was amiss, as is now clear from the archived papers of Wal Fife, the then junior minister responsible for the Bureau as part of the Department of Business and Consumer Affairs.

Fife's papers, now lodged with the National Library of Australia, reveal a file note Fife had received from Tim Besley, the permanent head of his department. This was dated 9 November, just days after the Cabinet of Prime Minister Malcolm Fraser decided to disband the Narcotics Bureau. Besley wrote that the department had started on the basis of a good relationship with the royal commission, and that Mr Justice Williams in particular 'regarded the Narcotics Bureau as an efficient and effective unit'. But in spite of Besley's offer to provide experienced officers to assist Williams, none was chosen; instead, some sixteen officers of the Commonwealth Police Force and two Queensland Police Force officers made up the royal commission's investigative force.

Besley also noted that at some stage 'something had changed' when a letter adverse to the Bureau was received from Hampson:

> The Hampson letter, in the main, contained general allegations with no supporting evidence. It indicated that the Commission had received evidence from unstated sources which led to the formulation by it of general conclusions on which it invited us to comment. We did so as fully as we were able in light of the general nature of the letter [...] I must say that during the sittings in Brisbane the attitude towards me and my colleagues was decidedly hostile.

Because of this hostility, the department had engaged counsel for those sittings where Bureau operations were under examination. As Besley noted, 'I did my best to get the Commission to give me something tangible to go on. But this was not forthcoming. I felt as though I was "punching" a feather bag.' The Besley note went further to describe his concerns about corruption in departments other than the Narcotics Bureau:

> I have to say I am disturbed at the apparent connection between the Royal Commission and the Queensland

Police. It is a fact that during sittings in Brisbane, Queensland police witnesses gave false evidence in respect of Tewantin. It is also a fact that the judge's report is silent on this. The Leader of the Opposition [Bill Hayden], a former Queensland police officer, has been alleging corruption of the Narcotics Bureau and has implied that his source is the Queensland police. Added to this there is also the possible Lewis, Murphy, Hallahan connection.

At the time the Williams royal commission had started its work, there were leaks to newspapers from Queensland police 'sources' critical of the Bureau. It was reported that, during in-camera hearings at the commission, a Commonwealth police officer had declared the Narcotics Bureau was 'totally inept', and that Bureau officers were not capable of presenting matters in court. One report claimed, again from unnamed 'sources', that the Bureau had on its staff an officer on the payroll of the 'Mr Asia' drug syndicate couriers Douglas and Isabel Wilson.

Serious reputational damage to the Bureau was being done. The 'Tewantin' Besley referred to, as Shobbrook has explained, was an apparently contrived drugs raid by Queensland police on a house at Werin Street. Its intention, it appears, was to show the Narcotics Bureau as incompetent, lazy or corrupt. Would Queensland police at the time have had the audacity to stage-manage such a raid, including planting drugs in the Tewantin house and making associated patsy arrests, all under the watchful eye of Commissioner Williams, for the purpose of discrediting the Narcotics Bureau?

In any event, serious doubts were being raised about the Bureau's effectiveness. On 7 August 1979, Prime Minister Fraser wrote to Commissioner Williams about considering improvements to the Narcotics Bureau, but, as Shobbrook describes, Williams response in an interim report six weeks later was to strongly recommend that the Bureau be disbanded.

As Shobbrook points out, Williams's interim report provided no reference to or finding of any corruption, or even of a suspicion of it, within the Bureau. Instead, the report offered the commissioner's opinion that the Bureau was not a 'highly efficient' enforcement agency, that there was 'considerable and increasing distrust' among other enforcement bodies and 'within the judicial system generally speaking', that its reputation for efficiency was 'lower' than that of state police, and that the Bureau had demonstrated itself 'overly sensitive' in its dealings with other agencies.

Fife's parliamentary papers reveal he and others put up a fight before the Cabinet's ultimate decision to accept Williams's recommendation, and for the Bureau's resources to be merged with the newly formed AFP. But Fife was a junior minister and not in the room when Cabinet submissions and options were debated. On 1 November 1979, Fife sent a letter to Fraser rebutting Williams's interim report. Fraser was made aware of the arrest of Milligan and its context. Fife also told Fraser that Harvey Bates was aware of a concerted effort to denigrate the Bureau, and that 'Milligan appeared to be in possession of knowledge which suggested that senior officers of the

Queensland Police were involved in criminal activity'.

Bates proposed a joint investigation of Milligan's allegations with Sir Colin Wood, the inaugural commissioner of the AFP. This course of action was raised by Tim Besley, but Wood 'felt unable' to agree to a joint investigation. A briefing note Fife and his department prepared to accompany their Cabinet submission concerning the disbanding recommendation declared the interim report 'was selective, subjective and open to challenge on almost every point'.

Nevertheless, the axe fell on the Bureau on 6 November 1979, Melbourne Cup Day. A cynic may conclude that this day was selected as the nation's attention was elsewhere. For the Fraser Cabinet to make such a momentous decision as disbanding the Bureau, in the face of confidential concerns about corrupt influence, would indicate the failure of preparatory staff work by the the secretary of the Department of Prime Minister and Cabinet, Sir Geoffrey Yeend.

What happened next could have been an opportunity for the Williams royal commission to get back on track and identify criminals and organisations trafficking in drugs. But, tragically, it had the opposite effect. According to Shobbrook, on 7 November 1979, while he was in Canberra being briefed about the consequences of the Cabinet decision, his Operation Jungle colleague John Moller, reeling from the smearing of the Bureau in the media, made allegations of police and political corruption in Queensland to Brisbane talkback radio station 4IP. These remarks were then published in *The Courier-Mail*, and there was immediate public controversy.

In a put-up-or-shut-up parliamentary manoeuvre, Premier Bjelke-Petersen provoked opposition leader Ed Casey and his MPs into naming four politicians under parliamentary privilege. There was no specific detail of their alleged wrongdoing, only the fact that the MPs had been 'named' in police records of interview with criminals. Casey explained that he was not alleging the MPs were involved in the drug trade, but he said he was recounting allegations made to him by a former Narcotics Bureau investigator, who based the information on a taped interview by convicted drug criminal John Edward Milligan. Premier Bjelke-Petersen then wrote to Commissioner Williams, asking that the allegations be investigated.

His terms of reference thus extended, Williams instructed the Brisbane office of the Narcotics Bureau to supply him with all intelligence that named any Queensland police or politicians. The Milligan Tapes and the brief of evidence Shobbrook had compiled on Milligan and Hallahan were packaged up and sent to the royal commission.

The new phase of the investigation started on 3 January 1980. In *The Most Dangerous Detective* (self-published in 2012 and updated in 2015), investigative journalist Steve Bishop shows how Williams and Hampson, without compunction, applied adversarial defensive tactics to bury Milligan and his evidence – and, in consequence, Shobbrook and his fellow Bureau investigators. Instead of laying out the factual substance of Milligan's incriminating information, Hampson put the police allegations to one side and concentrated on the MPs. Shobbrook was always unconcerned about the MPs Milligan named in the course of the taped conversations, as there was no direct evidence of their involvement in drug importation operations. The substance of evidence leading from Milligan's self-incrimination primarily concerned Hallahan and his police connections.

The Williams royal commission report, released in April 1980, exonerated the named MPs, as well as Lewis and Murphy. On Hallahan, it declared that the evidence fell 'far short' of establishing Hallahan's involvement in drug trafficking, and Williams argued that it was appropriate for him to comment on the allegations made against Hallahan:

> The officers of the Australian Federal Police, Narcotics Operations, have not concluded investigations into the association between Hallahan and Milligan and into the question of involvement by Hallahan in wrong-doing. The fact that these investigations have not concluded makes the Commission very reluctant to embark upon an analysis of all the evidence relating to Hallahan and his associating with Milligan. A public discussion of this evidence would very likely impede such investigations and would almost certainly be inimical to a fair trial if in fact the investigations resulted in a charge of some kind or other being laid against Hallahan. The Commission merely records that the evidence presently available to it falls far short of establishing as even a reasonable possibility, that Hallahan has ever been involved in wrong-doing in connection with illegal drugs.

This, then, was the cover-up. The extensive evidence against Hallahan remains in the confidential exhibits, now a sealed crypt, with a covering report by Justice Williams.

Steve Bishop's exhaustive deconstruction of the cover-up considerably damaged Hampson's reputation. Bishop had tried to interview Hampson, but the QC said he had burnt all his commission papers and could no longer recollect the details. Bishop published his extensive book 'knowing [Hampson] could sue me for libel, but no writ arrived'.

As you have read, a disillusioned Shobbrook got on with his life after having been invalided out of the police. He was deeply hurt by the Williams commission's smear of his professional competence, particularly since his work, and that of his Bureau colleagues, did result in the legislated remit of his agency: the conviction of a drug importer.

Shobbrook kept the detailed paperwork of his police file from Operation Jungle for decades until a bushfire at his Coonabarabran home destroyed much of it. The signatories of the letters patent establishing the Williams royal commission into drugs, the Commonwealth, Queensland, Tasmanian, Western Australian and Victorian governments, all owe John Shobbrook and his supportive colleagues of the Federal Bureau of Narcotics a formal apology for the cover-up administered by Williams and Hampson. We need to reconcile with Shobbrook for the sake of human decency, at the very least.

A royal commission nowadays can apply extraordinary coercive powers – undercover surveillance, wire taps and full evidentiary discovery, for example – to overcome any forensic disadvantage when confronted with a liar or calculated perjurer out to flout an oath to tell the truth, the whole truth and nothing but the truth. In the New South Wales Independent Commission Against Corruption's public hearings, individuals under examination have sometimes found themselves confronted with audio and video surveillance material that has immediately exposed their lies and imaginative denials. For those commissions of inquiry that find themselves boxed in by too narrow terms of reference, it is always possible for a commissioner to apply to extend the brief in the public interest. Under public scrutiny, it should be difficult for any government to refuse such an application.

In an article published in *Griffith Review* in 2019, the now retired Gary Crooke QC set out the changes by which the ground-breaking inquiries in which he participated more effectively pursued their terms of reference.* Crooke wrote that Gibbs's National Hotel royal commission had been bound by the 'Six Salmon Principles' established by the English Lord Salmon. These set down procedural fairness for witnesses and anyone adversely affected, with their legal representation encouraged, normally at public expense. But these procedures were adversarial, not inquisitorial, and in 1987, Fitzgerald seized the moment to seek change. As Crooke writes:

> The Queensland *Commissions of Inquiry Act* was archaic in content, having been untouched for many decades [...]

---

* Crooke, G. 2019, 'Unmasking a Culture of Corruption: Reflections on the Fitzgerald inquiry', *Griffith Review*, No. 65, pp. 43–52.

Fitzgerald – with great prescience, and departing greatly from established precedent – requested wholesale amendments to the Act to make it an effective instrument to conduct an investigative inquiry. Importantly, there was a significant departure from the concept enshrined in the Six Salmon Principles that greatly mirrored the trappings of adversarial litigation.

Another factor giving rise to Fitzgerald's ultimate success was that Mike Ahern's state government itself was represented at the inquiry, and was instrumental in assisting Fitzgerald to expose both political and police corruption. As Crooke says, 'Undoubtedly the inquiry and its report led to a change in government. This outcome was fully anticipated by Premier Mike Ahern, who made it clear that it was his duty to accept and implement the inquiry recommendations to make a better future for Queensland.'

In future, those prime ministers, premiers and chief ministers who want to sool a royal commission or commission of inquiry onto an issue, political rival, institution, corporation, industry or individual should think deeply about their own motivations. Public trust and the public good are at stake. These inquiries can so easily be misused for partisan, whitewash or cover-up purposes. Those considering taking up appointment as commissioners or joining the legally qualified or investigative staff should reflect on the integrity they must uphold and intellectual honesty they must display in accepting any appointment. The public interest should be the only motivation for engagement with such a powerful entity.

Further, governments themselves should consider being represented to assist inquiries in which their own governance and bureaucracies are to be examined. Such government participation was, in part, a major reason for the success of the Royal Commission into Institutional Responses to Child Sexual Abuse (2013–2017). That commission, established by Prime Minister Julia Gillard, joined the Commonwealth with all states and territories as signatories. It was a journey into the truth that was of great therapeutic benefit for victims, and presented a lasting lesson to institutions: when it comes to child sexual abuse, your institution's reputation is of no importance. Call the police immediately.

The Centre for Public Integrity, a not-for-profit organisation headed by Tony Fitzgerald QC with governance by former judicial officers and lawyers, and crowd-funded through transparent donations from the concerned citizens of Australia, was established in 2019 (see www.publicintegrity.org.au). The centre collaborates with academic experts, legal practitioners and retired judges to conduct research on critical integrity reform. It has posted an integrity reform agenda with research publications to begin the hard process of changing our attitudes to restore public trust in our liberal democracy, our laws and our institutions.

The centre is currently seeking public support for the establishment of an independent and adequately funded and resourced National Integrity Commission, which would investigate allegations and expose misconduct in the Commonwealth government and public sector. It hopes to educate the Australian public about the regrettable necessity of making sure our democracy functions for the public good. The Centre for Public Integrity stands ready to constructively critique and support anyone engaged in the difficult task of law enforcement and accountability.

The handling of Operation Jungle and its aftermath now stand as a salutary lesson in what not to do.

Author's Note

THE EVENTS DESCRIBED IN this book took place forty years ago but are not recounted from memory. I entered the Williams royal commission as a cooperative witness but was quickly accused of fabricating evidence. Fearing that a trumped-up charge could be laid against me – in the interests of self-preservation and to prove my innocence – I copied and retained key documents from my Operation Jungle dossier (a dossier that could 'disappear' at any time).

Shortly after leaving the Narcotics Bureau/Australian Federal Police (AFP), I supplied journalist Steve Bishop with a wealth of documentation to assist him in writing his book, *The Most Dangerous Detective*. Then, in 2013, I lost my home, and the documentation that I held, in a bushfire. Fortunately, after the bushfire Steve Bishop returned to me the folder of documentation that I had given to him in the 1980s.

This documentation contained royal commission transcripts, reports prepared by me for the royal commission, correspondence with Senator Don Chipp, criminal records, newspaper articles, internal Narcotics Bureau reports, handwritten notes taken at the time, the Operation Jungle timeline, correspondence between myself and the AFP, correspondence with former Leader of the Opposition in Queensland Wayne Goss, Statement of Service and Specialist Training Courses, correspondence with the Commonwealth Employees' Compensation organisation, the royal commission's list of public and confidential exhibits, and a Record of Interview between myself and John Milligan.

This book wasn't written after forty years, but over forty years. Some of the dialogue that I have quoted may not be word for word, but the content is accurate and the words included here don't fall wide of the mark.

After severing ties with the Australian Federal Police, I drove a school bus for special-needs children, then took up voluntary work at a local primary school, following which I worked in the computer department at a secondary college in Brisbane. In my spare time I discovered an interest in astronomy and built two observatories for the college in Brisbane. Eventually I ran 'Astronomy Days of Excellence' for students throughout South East Queensland.

In 1994, my family and I moved to Coonabarabran, in north-western New South Wales, which allowed me to work at Siding Spring Observatory, and in 1997 I was elected as a Fellow of the Royal Astronomical Society and a member of the Astronomical Society of Australia. In August 1998, we moved to California, where I became director of the Palmdale School District Planetarium, but my family and I grew homesick and returned to Coonabarabran and the Siding Spring Observatory in 2000. In 2001, Asteroid Shobbrook 148604 (2001 RO63), which orbits the Sun every 4.32 years with an absolute magnitude of 15.9, was named in honour of my role in astronomy education.

After the stress of the Narcotics Bureau and Williams royal commission years, and living on the edge of Los Angeles, returning to the Australian countryside was a slice of heaven. But heaven turned to hell on 13 January 2013, when my home was destroyed by a bushfire. I remain a crusading investigator, and have recently taken up the cause of farmers who were not compensated after their homes and properties were destroyed by a bushfire that escaped from an unpatrolled national park.

Acknowledgements

QUENTIN DEMPSTER HAS KNOWN of my story since the Fitzgerald inquiry days of the mid-1980s. Occasionally I would contact Quentin when faced with a specific problem – nobody offered me such prompt, detailed and sound advice as did Quentin. It was he who put my manuscript on the path to publication. A personal thank you for your important contribution to this book and your friendship over the years.

Matthew Condon has always offered support and encouragement as what was described by him as my 'extraordinary unpublished memoir' morphed into this book. I am humbled to have stood upon your shoulders, Matthew, and to have your name on the cover as a contributor.

Steve Bishop. A friend, fearless reporter and a researcher without peer as exemplified in his book, *The Most Dangerous*

Detective. If Steve hadn't retained the documents that I had sent to him in the early 1980s then my book would not exist. Steve, whose knowledge of the disbanding of the Narcotics Bureau is encyclopaedic, is another giant upon whose shoulders I stood.

I took strength to comment with censure on Sir Edward Williams QC from his fellow Queensland Supreme Court Judge James Thomas AM QC. I was staggered as I read Judge Thomas's book *An Almost Forgotten World*, which confirmed that my opinions of Justice Williams's character weren't fanciful.

Paul Giamatti. To have a Golden Globe–winning and Academy Award–nominated actor and producer show such interest that he came to my home to discuss the Operation Jungle story with me was an incredible motivator for me to turn my story into hard copy. Thanks to you and Hoke Moseley for your encouragement.

To have a literary giant such as Richard Walsh take the time to read and then polish my original manuscript was such an honour. Richard was incredibly generous with his advice and a recommendation from him led to my publisher.

To Madonna Duffy, Felicity Dunning, Kate McCormack, Sally Wilson, Madeline Byrne and the wonderful and caring team at the University of Queensland Press. What an honour to be in your company.

Julian Welch, my editor. Your in-depth understanding of what the book was about, your wisdom and your patience as you showed me how to turn a collection of facts into a smooth-flowing narrative is greatly appreciated.

Brian Bennett and Denis Gray. Two Narcotics Bureau

colleagues of uncompromising integrity. The role model that the late Brian Bennett presented as I worked alongside him enabled me to develop into the investigator that I became. In the same mould, Denis patiently played the role of sounding board as this book was written. Two additional colleagues cannot be overlooked – John Moller and Noel Caswell. Sincerest thanks for the first-class investigation that led, at a time of considerable upheaval, to three arrests and three guilty pleas.

To my former colleagues from the Federal Bureau of Narcotics. For decades you have been wrongly and spitefully cast as corrupt or at the very least incompetent investigators. Your careers and lives suffered as a consequence. It is too late to repair the damage done by the baseless disbanding of the Bureau, but I hope that this book at least sets the record straight. It is long overdue for the Federal Government to send a letter of apology to those agents who are still alive and to the families of those who have passed away. Thank you for your fellowship and for remaining true.

To Steph Venturato at the State Library of Queensland and to the indefatigable Jim Slade – thank you each for your amazing assistance with my research.

On a personal level, she doesn't want me to, but how can I fail to mention my wife, Jan. Jan joined the Narcotics Bureau in Brisbane before I joined in Sydney. She either knew personally, or knew of, most of the cast of characters mentioned in this book and shared in the distress that I went through. They hurt her as much as they hurt me. Jan, my love and admiration for you leaves me speechless, sentiments that I also hold for our children, Vanessa and Doug.

Where Are They Now?

JOHN MILLIGAN

After serving six years in custody for his Operation Jungle conviction, John Edward Milligan was released from Long Bay Gaol on 24 January 1986. He allegedly travelled to the Philippines, and his parole was revoked on 30 March 1986, when it was claimed that he had broken one of the conditions of his release. In October 1986, Milligan was charged with possession and supply of 17 grams of heroin. He never faced court on this charge, having absconded while on bail. Milligan died on 3 December 1993, aged forty-nine, but there are no details about his death listed in the Australian Cemeteries Index. He is buried in the Tweed Heads Lawn Cemetery in New South Wales.

IAN BARRON

Ian Robert Barron pleaded guilty to a charge of Conspiracy

to Import a Prohibited Import and was sentenced to five years' imprisonment.

GRAHAM BRIDGE

Graham David Bridge pleaded guilty to a charge of Conspiracy to Import a Prohibited Import and was sentenced to five years' imprisonment.

BRYAN PARKER

Bryan William Parker was never arrested for his involvement in the Jane Table Mountain importation. He died in the Royal Prince Alfred Hospital in Sydney on 11 August 1979 from a rheumatic heart condition before the Operation Jungle investigation progressed sufficiently for him to be interviewed and arrested.

ROBERT ALTHAUS

Robert Althaus, who also went by the name Robert Harvey, was never interviewed or charged with any offence concerning the Jane Table Mountain heroin importation. I believe the AFP took no further interest in him once I had left the organisation.

GLEN HALLAHAN

Glendon Patrick Hallahan's career as a sweet corn farmer was relatively short-lived. In 1986, he filed for bankruptcy, listing debts of $180,118 and cash in hand of $100. On 13 January 1986, the Queensland Government, still under the premiership of Sir Joh Bjelke-Petersen, appointed Hallahan as the Chief Claims Investigator for the state government's insurance company, Suncorp. They made this appointment without advertising the position or calling for any other applications. Hallahan's good character was attested to by none other than Sir Terence Lewis. Hallahan died of cancer in Brisbane on 17 June 1991. He is buried in Beenleigh Cemetery, south of Brisbane.

TERRY LEWIS

Terence Murray Lewis received a number of awards in recognition of his service during his law-enforcement career: he received the Queen's Police Medal in 1977; he was made an Officer of the British Empire in June 1979; on New Year's Day 1986, he was made a Knight Bachelor for his service to the Queensland police; and on 15 May 1986 he was awarded the National Medal, recognising that he had put himself at risk in the service of the community, or in the course of enforcing the law to protect persons or property.

After being heavily criticised in the Fitzgerald inquiry's final report, Lewis was stood down as police commissioner in 1987 and charged with various offences in 1989. He was found guilty by a Brisbane District Court jury in 1991 and jailed for fourteen years for fifteen corruption charges, and ten years for a forgery charge. In March 1993, Lewis became only the fourteenth person since the fourteenth century to be stripped of his knighthood. Lewis was paroled in 2002 after serving ten and a half years. He continued to protest his innocence, suing his former lawyers and pursuing further appeals, the last of which failed in August 2005.

TONY MURPHY

In March 1982, Tony Murphy issued a writ for defamation against the ABC, which had claimed that Murphy had been a member of the allegedly corrupt Rat Pack since the 1960s. Murphy's writ named forty-three men who would vouch for his honesty. The Fitzgerald inquiry found that of those forty-three, '[t]here were at least nine against whom there was evidence of serious corruption in this inquiry ... two others who confessed to corruption during this inquiry, about four against whom allegations of perjury have been made, and five others against whom other serious allegations of misconduct have been made'. What 'honest cop' would ask a bent copper for a reference? And what bent copper would give a reference to an honest cop? As Aesop put it, a man is known by the company he keeps.

Murphy retired in December 1982 at the rank of assistant commissioner, and was granted the licence to run the Stradbroke Island TAB agency. He died in December 2010, aged eighty-three.

EDWARD STRATTEN WILLIAMS

Ned Williams became Sir Edward in 1981, when he was created a Knight Commander of the British Empire, and again in 1983, as a Knight Commander of Saint Michael and Saint George. In 1982, he received the Australian of the Year award, and shared the dais at the Brisbane Commonwealth Games Opening Ceremony with Queen Elizabeth II and Prince Philip. In 1983, he was awarded the title of Queenslander of the Year, and became head of the

National Crimes Commission. A horse race named after him, the Sir Edward Williams Handicap, in previous years run on Queensland Oaks Day at Eagle Farm racecourse, has had its name changed. Williams was a member of the International Narcotics Control Board from 1982 to 1987, and between 1993 and 1996 he served as a judge of the Court of Appeal of Fiji. He died on 10 January 1999 and is buried in Nudgee Cemetery, Brisbane.

CEDRIC EDWARD KEID HAMPSON

A year after his appointment as Counsel Assisting the Williams royal commission, Cedric Hampson QC was appointed President of the Queensland Bar Association. He held that role until 1981, and again from 1995 to 1996. From 1983 until his retirement in 2006 he was a leader of the Queensland Bar. Hampson was also active in the affairs of the Catholic Church, as Queensland Lieutenant of the Equestrian Order of the Holy Sepulchre of Jerusalem, and as a Knight of the Order of Saint Lazarus of Jerusalem. In January 1984, for his contribution to the Williams and Stewart royal commissions, Hampson was appointed an Officer of the Order of Australia. In 2012, Pope Benedict XVI awarded him a Knighthood of the Order of Saint Gregory the Great. Hampson died in 2014, and is buried in Nudgee Cemetery, Brisbane. Brisbane's Cedric Hampson Chambers is named in his honour.

Further Reading

'18-year Term on Drug Counts', *Telegraph* (Brisbane), 20 March 1980, p. 1.

'Bates Back as Bureau Head', *The Canberra Times*, 5 June 1979, p. 1.

Bishop, S. 2015, *The Most Dangerous Detective: The Outrageous Glen Patrick Hallahan*, 2nd Ed., Self-published.

'Bitter with Drug Report', *Telegraph* (Brisbane), 18 April 1980, p. 5.

Chipp, D. 1982, Address to the Australian Senate, 25 March.

Condon, M. 2014, *Jacks and Jokers*, University of Queensland Press, Brisbane.

Dickie, P., 'Milligan's Mountain', *The Courier-Mail*, 9 August 1988.

Fitzgerald, T. 1989, *Report to the Queensland Government on the alleged involvement in the illegal drug trade by Queensland*

Parliamentarians and Senior Police, Government Printer, Brisbane.

Fraser, M. 1977, Parliamentary Debates House of Representatives – National Drug Inquiry, Ministerial Statement, 5 October, p. 1659.

'Marihuana Seized in Swoop by Police on Weirdos', *Sunday Truth* (Brisbane), 11 August 1963, p. 1.

'The Moonlight State' 1987, *Four Corners*, television broadcast, 11 May, ABC, Australia. Written by C. Masters.

Parliamentary Papers of Wal Fife, 1942–2001, MS7626, National Library of Australia, Canberra.

'Politicians Linked to Drug Rings', *The Courier-Mail*, 8 November 1979, p. 1.

Stewart, D.G. 1983, *Report of the Royal Commission of Inquiry into Drug Trafficking (Australia)*, Government Printer, Sydney.

'Text of Federal Police statement on drugs', *The Canberra Times*, 11 December 1979, p. 10.

Thomas, J.B. 2011, *An Almost Forgotten World: Jim Thomas's Memoirs*, Supreme Court of Queensland Library, Brisbane.

Williams, E.S. 1979, *Interim Report of the Australian Royal Commission of Inquiry into Drugs; of the government of the Commonwealth of Australia and the governments of the states of Victoria, Queensland, Western Australia and Tasmania*, Government Printer, Brisbane.

Woodward, P.M. 1979, *Report of the Royal Commission into Drug Trafficking*, Government Printer, Sydney.